The Painted House of Maud Lewis

The Painted House of Maud Lewis

Conserving a Folk Art Treasure

Laurie Hamilton

Goose Lane Editions
Art Gallery of Nova Scotia

Edited by Dianne O'Neill.
Cover photographs: detail of the storm door, Laurie Hamilton;
Maud Lewis © Bob Brooks Illustrative Photography.
Printed in Canada by Friesens.
10 9 8 7

National Library of Canada Cataloguing in Publication Data

Hamilton, Laurie E., 1950-
The painted house of Maud Lewis: conserving a folk art treasure
Issued also in French under title: La maison peinte de Maud Lewis.
Co-published by: Art Gallery of Nova Scotia.
Includes bibliographical references and index.
ISBN 0-86492-334-1

1. Lewis, Maud, 1903-1970 — Homes and haunts — Nova Scotia.
2. Historic buildings — Conservation and restoration — Nova Scotia.
3. Mural painting and decoration — Conservation and restoration — Nova Scotia.
4. Folk art — Conservation and restoration — Nova Scotia.
I. Art Gallery of Nova Scotia II. Title.

ND249.L447H35 2001 759.11 C2001-902375-8

Goose Lane Editions acknowledges the generous financial support of the Government of Canada, the Canada Council for the Arts, and the Province of New Brunswick. The Art Gallery of Nova Scotia is grateful for the support of the Department of Tourism and Culture, Province of Nova Scotia, the Department of Canadian Heritage, the Museums Assistance Program, the Art Gallery of Nova Scotia Gallery Shop, and Scotiabank.

Goose Lane Editions
500 Beaverbrook Court, Suite 330
Fredericton, New Brunswick
CANADA E3B 5X4
gooselane.com

Art Gallery of Nova Scotia
1723 Hollis Street
Halifax, Nova Scotia
CANADA B3J 3C8
artgalleryofnovascotia.ca

Contents

This House

This house, from where you watched the world go by
This house, touched here and there with childhood's eyes
Every surface your blank page, a self-painted gilded cage,
with bluebirds flying free
Painted flowers on the stair, blooming everywhere,
now here for all to see
Within this house

These hands, they could only do so much
These hands, curled and spent around the brush
Did you paint away the pain, paint away the tears,
and the misery
While painting stories from the past, times that did not last,
childhood's memories
With these hands

These eyes, witness to the passing ways
These eyes, now glancing from a stranger's gaze
They saw the oxen and the cart, they were the window
to your heart, open wide enough to breathe

Painting brightly coloured scenes, pictures found in dreams,
you alone could see
With these eyes

This house, now silent witness to your life
This house, once fraught with hardship and with life
Yet does it guard unspoken dreams, preserve silent memories,
unseen by curious eyes
Quietly waiting for the brush, your loving tender touch,
to caress it one more time . . .

— Dan McKinnon, 4 June 1998

Dan McKinnon is a singer/songwriter based in Halifax, Nova Scotia. He composed this song for the opening of the Scotiabank Maud Lewis Gallery and recorded it on his CD, Songs from the Hearth.

Foreword

Following the death of Everett Lewis in 1979, Maud Lewis's tiny house fell into disrepair and deteriorated quickly. A group of local citizens formed the Maud Lewis Painted House Society. Led by René Richard, the Society worked diligently to raise funds to acquire, preserve, and display the House as a lasting tribute to Maud Lewis. The Society approached me for assistance in 1979, and together we arranged for the Canadian Conservation Institute to carry out an analysis of the structure.

By 1983, the society determined that there was insufficient financial support in the community to bring their project to fulfilment, and in 1984 the house, its contents, and the property were purchased by the Province of Nova Scotia for the Art Gallery of Nova Scotia. Ideally, any cultural object should be displayed *in situ*, but when this became impossible, we decided to move the whole structure into storage. The Nova Scotia Department of Supply and Services subsequently moved the Maud Lewis Painted House from its Marshalltown site and placed it in a storage hangar in Waverley, near Halifax, Nova Scotia, pending its restoration and installation as an integral component of the gallery's permanent collection.

At that time, the Art Gallery of Nova Scotia did not have a permanent home itself. A proposal for a new building on the Halifax waterfront that incorporated a space specifically designed for the Maud Lewis Painted House gave way to the renovation of our heritage building on Hollis Street. Size limitations, however, did not allow the inclusion of Maud's house in this building as a permanent focus for our internationally recognized folk art collection. In 1993, the gallery established a special committee, chaired by Merv Russell, President of the Maritime Broadcasting Corporation, to raise funds for the conservation of the house, and adopted a five-year strategic plan that included a proposed expansion into an adjacent building which would house a gallery dedicated to Maud Lewis.

Concurrently, we worked with the Digby Board of Trade and with a local ad hoc committee, headed by Ken and Maxine Connell and assisted by Stephen Outhouse, on plans to establish a permanent memorial to Maud on the original Marshalltown site. In 1997, a memorial sculpture, designed by Brian MacKay-Lyons and fabricated by Cherubini Metalworks, was installed in a park environment designed by Tony Gillis. The memorial reflects simultaneously the simplicity of Maud's life and the joyous exuberance of her paintings. Its structural steel frame aptly conveys the greyness of Maud's life, while colour highlights suggest her childlike vision of the world. At the official dedication of the Maud Lewis Memorial, Reverend Ritchie McMurray noted that "Maud lived in deep poverty, yet managed to express outwardly in her art the beauty hidden in her soul."

As well, the gallery began planning a Maud Lewis exhibition that would tour nationally. Scotiabank announced its sponsorship of *The Illuminated Life of Maud Lewis* in 1995, and The Craig Foundation for the Visual and Performing Arts (now known as The Craig Foundation) confirmed its associate sponsorship a year later. More than half a million Canadians visited the exhibition in Halifax and across the country.

In 1996, Southwest Properties Limited, the managers of Sunnyside Mall in Bedford, Nova Scotia, provided a site where the preliminary stages of conservation treatment on the Maud Lewis Painted House could be undertaken in a situation that permitted interaction with

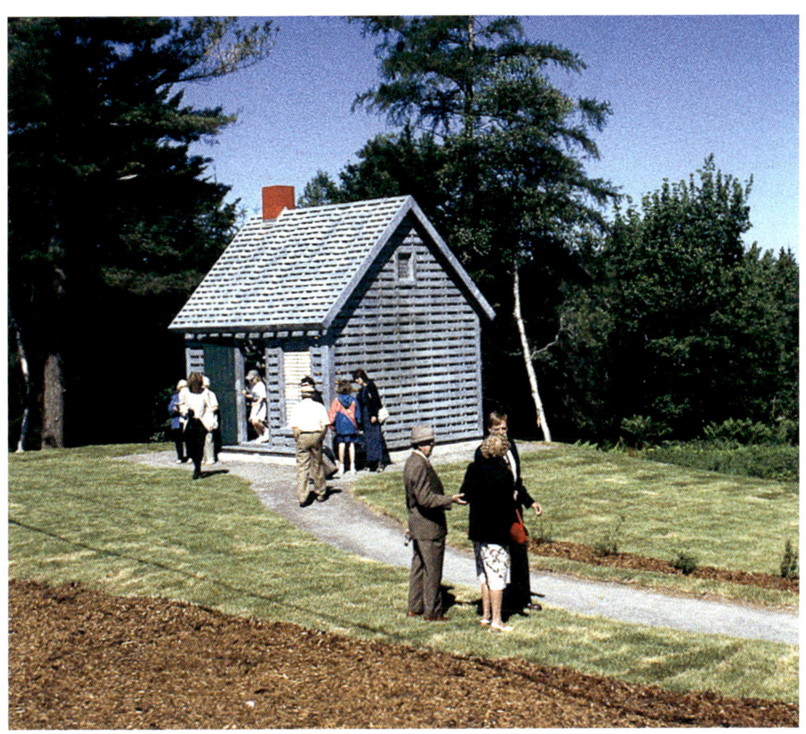

Maud Lewis Memorial Site, Marshalltown, on the day of the official opening, 4 July 1997. (Amirault Photography)

the public. At this time the Department of Canadian Heritage also provided generous support for the project through the Museums Assistance Program.

In 1997, Scotiabank solidified its association with Maud Lewis by endowing a permanent gallery in the AGNS Phase II Expansion. The Scotiabank Maud Lewis Gallery was officially opened in June, 1998, as a showcase for the creative talents of one of Canada's best loved folk artists. Here Maud's paintings, painted objects, and the fully restored Maud Lewis Painted House itself are permanently on display.

My congratulations and thanks are extended to AGNS Fine Art Conservator Laurie Hamilton, who supervised the overall restoration project and developed this important resource; she faced many challenges in developing the technical processes required to preserve this cultural treasure. Ably assisted by Jennifer McLaughlin and Craig Dix, she brought her high professional standards to bear on every aspect of the project.

Maud's door was always open to passersby. With her Painted House now on permanent display at the AGNS and a fitting memorial dedicated to her memory on the original site in Marshalltown, visitors can continue to marvel at the extraordinary life and work of this creative Nova Scotian folk artist for generations to come.

Bernard Riordon

Director and CEO
Art Gallery of Nova Scotia

Acknowledgements

For a project of this magnitude to come to fruition, extending as it did over a substantial period of time, the support of many people was required. I would like to thank the Director of the Art Gallery of Nova Scotia, Bernard Riordon, for his support and determination to see this preservation challenge through to its successful conclusion.

I am most grateful to my fellow conservators working in the private sector, without whom the restoration could never have been realized. Fine Art Conservator Jennifer McLaughlin brought skill and sensitivity to the conservation and restoration of the painted artifacts and was a joy to work with. My admiration and thanks go to Artifact Conservator Craig Dix and his crew, Todd Vassallo, Steve Shannon and Kim Jarrett, who gave new meaning to the phrase "team work."

I acknowledge with gratitude the financial support of the Department of Canadian Heritage, the Art Gallery of Nova Scotia Gallery Shop, Scotiabank, and the many individuals who donated what they could to help preserve the Maud Lewis Painted House.

To those who graciously permitted the use of photographs and archival material, Beth Brooks, Cora Greenaway, Livia Adalaar, Glenn Atchison, Charles Eisener, Amirault Photography, the Canadian Broadcasting Corporation, and the Canadian Conservation Institute, I am professionally and personally indebted.

For the donation of space, materials, expertise, or time, I want to thank the Nova Scotia Department of Lands and Forests, the management of Sunnyside Mall, Martha Crosby, the Davies sisters, Steve Roberts, and Finbar Tobin.

My sincere thanks are extended to my colleagues at the Art Gallery of Nova Scotia: to Judy Dietz, Manager of Gallery Services, for her discerning insights; to Virginia Stephen, former Deputy Director and Head of Programming, for her attention to the educational aspects of the project; to Brenda Garagan, Assistant to the Director, for her help with administrative details; to preparators Pat Beauchamp and Frank Lively, former preparator Bruce Campbell, and casual and contract staff Bob Scott, Matthew Collins, and Wilfred Miner for their assistance with the final installation. I am indebted to Dr. Dianne O'Neill, Associate Curator of Historical Prints and Drawings, for her superb editing skills and vast knowledge of things grammatical.

Finally, I wish to thank my husband David for providing much needed encouragement, advice, and occasional brawn, and to my children, Elizabeth and John, for their patience and understanding.

Laurie Hamilton
Fine Art Conservator
Art Gallery of Nova Scotia

Introduction

Many museums and galleries display elaborate period rooms which bring to life a historical era using the furnishings and accoutrements of daily life. The wonderful Croscup Room, now at the National Gallery of Canada but originally in a home in the village of Karsdale, Nova Scotia, features splendid nineteenth century plaster-wall paintings within the architectural framework of the original room setting. Private homes whose owners were avid

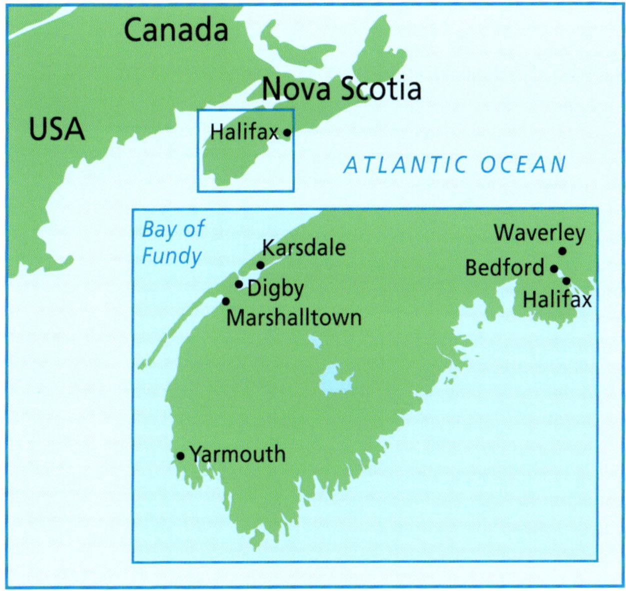

Map showing Karsdale, Digby, Marshalltown, Halifax, Bedford and Waverley.

collectors or noteworthy historical figures are often made into museums to house and display their particular collections or to animate the age in which the individuals lived. But this radical notion to install an entire house and its furnished interior as a "work of art" within the confines of an art gallery building is unique in the Canadian context. The remarkable nature of the Maud Lewis Painted House made this a realistic option. The fact that it functioned as home and studio for the artist over more than thirty years is interesting, but Maud's use of its walls and furnishings as the primary support for some of her early paintings makes it special, rare, and worthy of the time, effort, and money required to preserve it. The unusual display at the Art Gallery of Nova Scotia is the culmination of many factors, first and foremost of which was the pressing need to save the structure from the ravages of time. This book is designed to give some insight into the processes used to restore and conserve the Maud Lewis Painted House.

Everett Lewis acquired the house in 1926 and moved it by a team of oxen to Marshalltown, a small village on the outskirts of Digby, Nova Scotia. In 1938, Everett married Maud Dowley of Yarmouth County, and the tiny house became her home for the next thirty-two years, until her death in 1970. During this period, she transformed almost every surface of the simple rustic structure with her paintings, fulfilling her compelling need to express her love for the world around her on whatever surface was available. After Maud's death, Everett continued to live in the house, making a few alterations, until his demise in 1979. Individuals in the surrounding community formed the Maud Lewis Painted House Society, and their concerted effort to preserve the house on site continued through the following five years. Lack of funds and the realization that the house was deteriorating rapidly, however, forced members to seek an alternate approach. In the fall of 1984, the house was sold to the Province of Nova Scotia and turned over to the Art Gallery of Nova Scotia. There is always a measure of regret when an artifact is taken from its original surroundings, but those involved recognized that exposure to another winter might have tolled the death knell for the already weakened structure. Accordingly, the house was lifted from its foundation and moved as a single unit to a Nova Scotia Department of Lands and Forests storage hangar in Waverley, Nova Scotia.

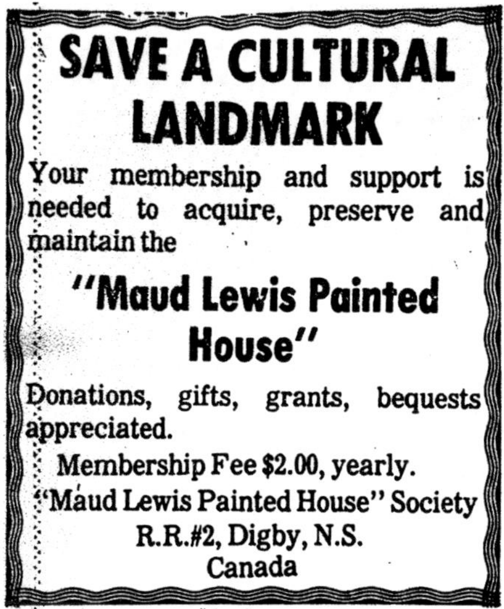

Original ad for membership in the Maud Lewis Painted House Society, April 1979.

Two critical circumstances united the public and private support that made a full restoration of the structure feasible. The first was the expansion of the Art Gallery of Nova Scotia into an adjacent building with space for a custom-designed gallery in which the Maud Lewis Painted House could be displayed. The second was financial support from two major sources: an endowment from Scotiabank for the Maud Lewis Gallery and grant money from the Museums Assistance Program, Department of Canadian Heritage, to offset some of the cost of the restoration procedures. At last, a permanent display of the Maud Lewis House could become a reality.

Seven major stages of documentation and treatment, roughly based on a chronological time-line, describe the restoration project: analysis of the condition of the house and its contents; research and documentation of the painted images; curatorial considerations for the final display; structural treatment of the house; treatment of the painted artifacts; research and treatment of the hand-painted wallpaper; and final installation details. In this book, the primary players give first-hand accounts of the expertise they brought to the successful completion of the project. Our story spans roughly two decades, beginning in the late 1970s, when Bernard Riordon, Director of the Art Gallery of Nova Scotia, first became involved, and ending with the opening of the Scotiabank Maud Lewis Gallery, featuring the fully restored house, in June of 1998. The story of the Maud Lewis Painted House, however, continues as each new visitor finds delight and inspiration in her joyous vision.

The life of Maud Lewis and the history of her painted house are well documented in the book, *The Illuminated Life of Maud Lewis*, by Lance Woolaver and Bob Brooks. The focus of *The Painted House of Maud Lewis* is on its painted decoration and the solutions formulated to treat a large, deteriorated wooden structure and to present it as a permanent installation in the Art Gallery of Nova Scotia. From rusted, structurally compromised breadboxes and brittle scraps of hand-painted wallpaper to wood spongy with rot, the project presented endless challenges and inspired a collaborative effort in conservators, curators, technicians, and preparators.

House Details and Condition

The Maud Lewis Painted House measures a scant 4.11 metres (13 feet 6 inches) along the front, 3.79 metres (12 feet 6 inches) along the side, and at its peak only 4.37 metres (14 feet 4 inches) high. Its southern orientation on the original property allowed the sun to enter the largest window on the front façade, where Maud sat and painted her small-scale paintings. Two smaller windows provided additional daylight, one on the west wall of the ground floor

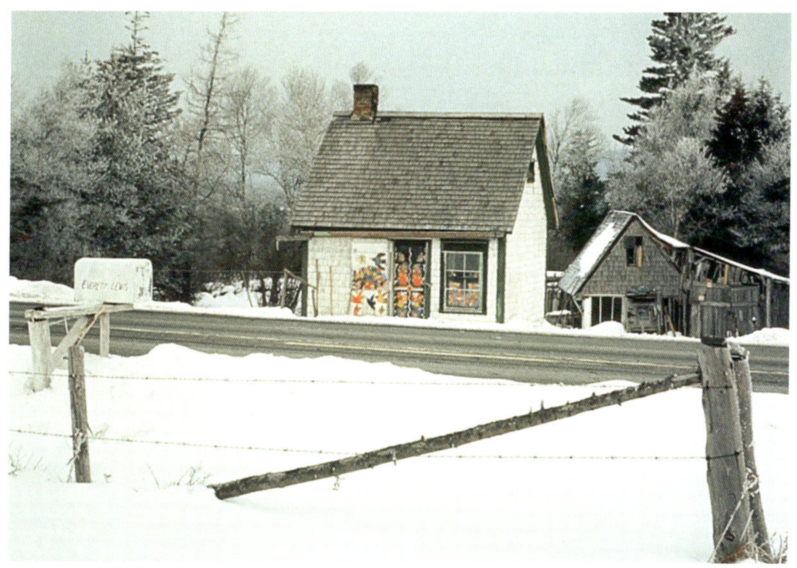

Maud Lewis Painted House at its original site in Marshalltown in 1965. (Bob Brooks)

and another in the attic, on the east gable end. The construction of the house is simple and its materials rough, many recycled from a former use. Coarsely hewn spruce shingles nailed to horizontal sheathing secured to studs, with little or no insulation to ward off the cold of winter or the heat of high summer, make up the exterior. Corner boards, fascia boards, and ridge caps, all typical features of wood construction, conceal and protect the various joints, as do trim boards around the door and windows. The wooden-shingled roof is pitched steeply to the front and back, and a brick chimney, situated near the west side of the house, penetrates the roof at the ridge cap. Cylindrical metal stove piping links it to the wood-burning stove below. Within the low concrete foundation, more evident at the back of the house on its original site, Maud and Everett could access cold storage space by an interior floor hatch. Metal strapping attaches a wooden eavestrough on the front elevation to the lower portion of the roof, sloping downwards to the west to allow water drainage. Two doors secure the single entranceway: a board and batten storm door swinging outwards and latched from the inside with large hook-and-eye hardware, and a panelled inner door with two small windows, swinging inward and equipped with a skeleton key lock.

The interior walls measure 1.82 metres (just under 6 feet) in height, with a plaster ceiling so low that Everett Lewis apparently had to tilt his head on a slight angle when standing. Horizontal wainscotting, composed of broad boards, covers the lower part of all four walls, extending up 79 centimetres (20 inches) from the floor, while rough plaster, keyed onto underlying lath, finishes the upper portion, approximately one metre in height. A rectangular opening into the back left corner of the ceiling, 95 by 65 centimetres (37½ by 25½ inches) gave Maud and Everett access up a steep staircase to the attic space. This area, with its sloping ceilings, served as sleeping quarters for the couple. Maud, however, was disabled with arthritis and eventually her disability forced her to remain on the ground floor. Everett scrounged a large wood-burning cookstove, manufactured by O.D. Clapp of Toledo, Ohio, which provided heat in the winter and cooking and baking capability year round. Sharp ninety-degree angles in the pipe linking stove to chimney made for a poor updraft and accounted for the large amount of soot found within the house. It was, no doubt, an unhealthy environment in which to live. The couple had neither running water nor electricity, and even when money was no longer an issue, Everett did nothing to upgrade the home. An exterior open well provided water, and coal oil lamps remained the source of illumination at night.

The single room was sparsely furnished, with shelving, tables, and chairs deployed along the walls. The massive stove took up most of the west wall, framed by some rough shelving that served as storage for dry goods and cooking utensils. Originally, a simple stepladder on the north wall gave access to the attic. This was replaced at a later date with a recycled staircase, presumably to make the climb easier for Maud as her arthritis worsened with passing years. It abutted a daybed, over which Everett had built more shelving and storage units, for the most part from converted wooden tea crates. They used these shelves for perishable goods since the cold, uninsulated northern exposure preserved food longer; there may also have been a box attached to the northern outside wall of the house, used for food storage. The east side of the room served as a combined dining area and office, with a drop-leaf table and more shelving. Here Maud piled the correspondence relating to her mail-order business, which flourished after the national publicity she received following the broadcast of a CBC-TV documentary and an article in the *Star Weekly*, both in 1965. The metal TV table, at which Maud painted during the daylight hours, was tucked into the south-east corner next to the big front window, through which she had a clear view of life passing by on the highway a short distance away.

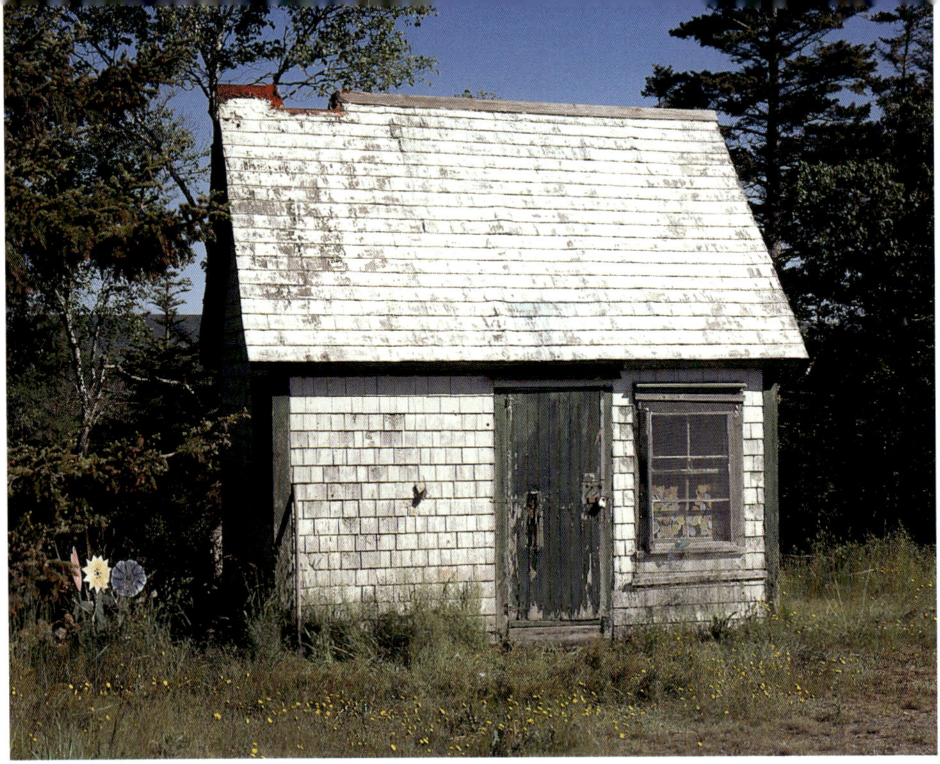

View of the House on site in Marshalltown in June 1984, five years after Everett's death, showing the condition of the exterior. (AGNS)

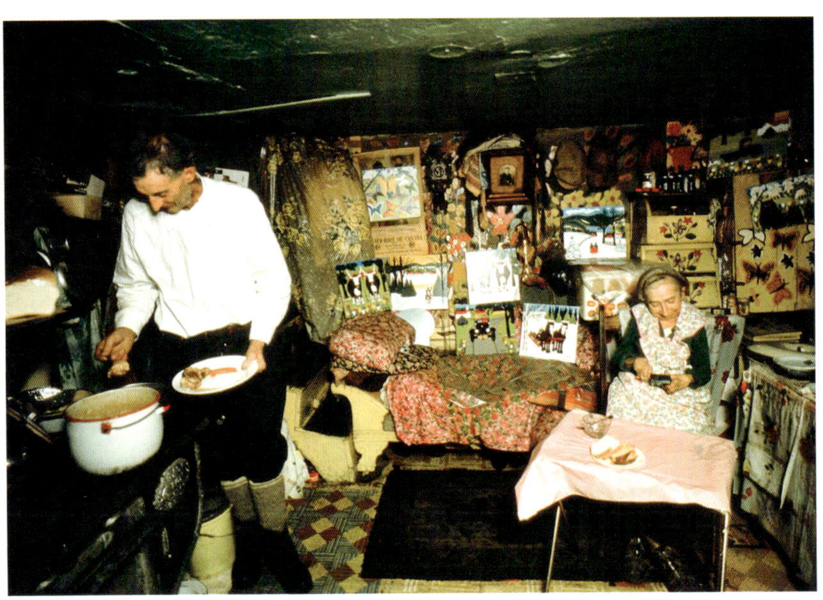

Interior view of the House with Maud and Everett in 1965. (Bob Brooks)

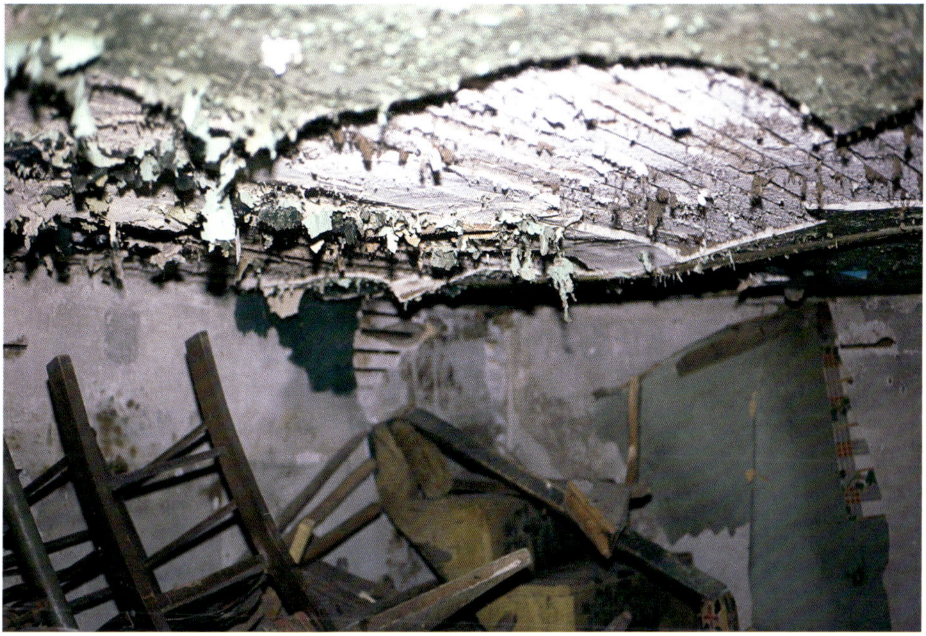

Detail showing the deterioration and extent of loss in the ceiling plaster. (AGNS)

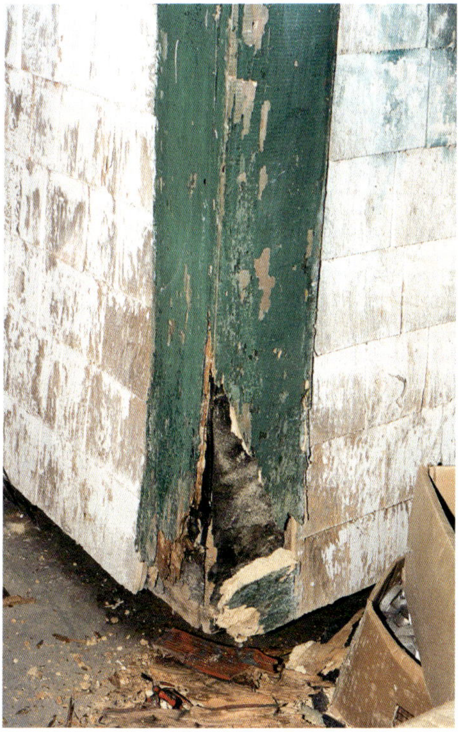

The lower sections of the House, in close proximity to the ground, suffered rot as a result of rising damp, as is seen in the corner boards prior to treatment. (Craig Dix)

Wooden kitchen-style chairs, none matching any other, provided adequate, if uncomfortable, seating.

The paraphernalia of everyday life cluttered the space throughout. Maud chose about twenty of these domestic utensils as surfaces on which to paint. Among the everyday objects to receive this special distinction were metal breadboxes and storage tins, cupboard doors, linoleum and oilcloth scraps, the warming oven, the stair risers, and even the wallpaper.

Condition Prior to Conservation Treatment

The fundamental structure of the house, composed primarily of wooden elements, was sound. There were certainly areas of rotting wood where close proximity to damp conditions had caused problems: the floor joists, window sill, door threshold and lower casings, and parts of the corner and fascia boards were all affected by rot. Insect infestation was also apparent in many sites — again, the lower elements of the house seemed most affected. The exterior spruce shingles, once painted white, had grown dirty, and overall loss of paint from weathering had exposed the bare wood beneath. Painted images of evergreen trees on the front facade, completed by Everett after Maud's death, were a faint vestige of what they had been in the early 1970s, victims of weathering and sun exposure. The roof shingles, painted white on the front and red on the back, were heavily soiled, and about half the paint no longer adhered to the wood beneath. Miraculously, the hand-painted window panes were unbroken and in excellent condition.

The interior of the house, however, was in an advanced state of deterioration. Fifty per cent of the ceiling plaster was missing, and the rest hung away from the lath above. The wall plaster had lost much of its key, and approximately twenty per cent was no longer in place.

Most distressing was the poor state of the hand-painted wallpaper on the north and east walls. Large segments were missing, and what remained was hanging away from the wall, sagged, torn, and dirty. Maud's wallpaper presented one of the major challenges of the restoration process. The metal objects, including the stove, were severely rusted and, in some cases, structurally compromised. Other painted materials, including paper, cardboard, linoleum, and wood, were in need of cleaning, stabilizing, and, in some cases, consolidation.

With so many variant components in need of treatment, and with the large-scale nature of the job, the project demanded a team of conservators with specialized knowledge, working in tandem with museum-trained technicians and preparators. Timing can be a critical factor in such a project. It was indeed fortunate that by 1996, the expertise essential to undertake all areas of conservation and restoration was locally available in Halifax, Nova Scotia. The Maud Lewis Painted House reclamation could proceed with a realistic budget and an achievable time-line.

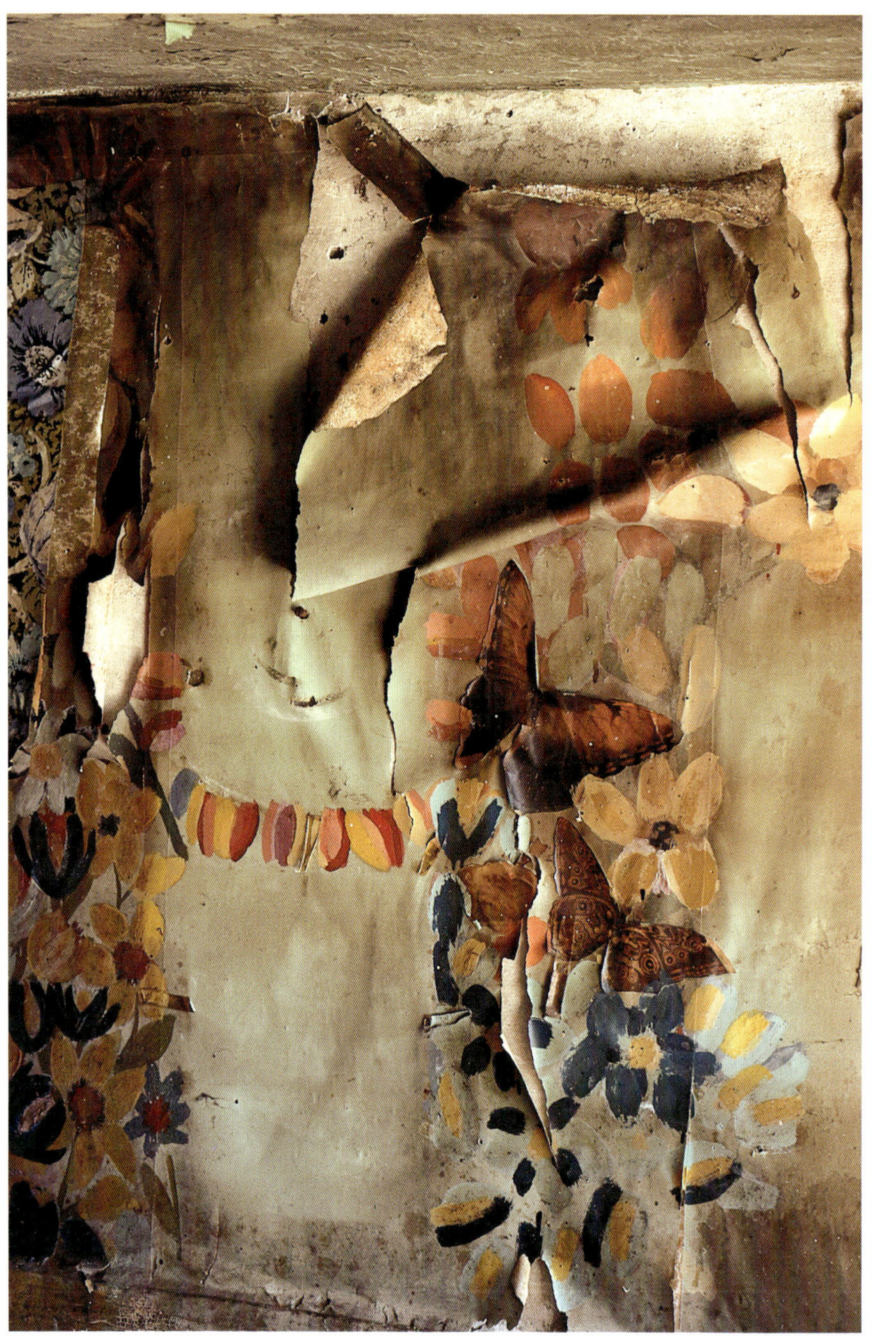

The condition of the wallpaper on the east wall prior to removal and treatment. (AGNS)

Maud's Images

The images the artist painted on the interior and exterior of the house provide insight into Maud's idiosyncratic vision, since they represent her early work, before she found herself on the commercial treadmill, producing small-scale paintings for a public clamouring for the same scenes over and over again. As described

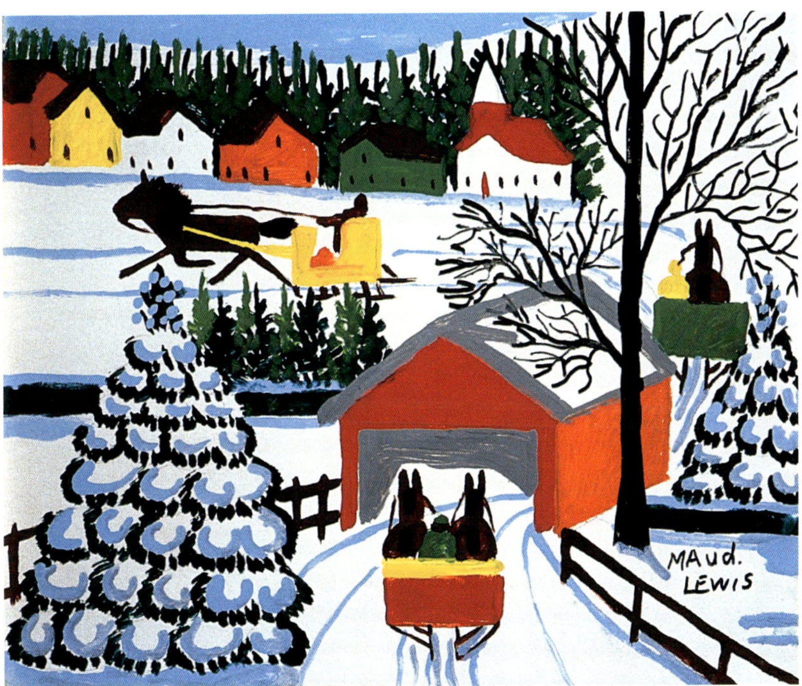

A typical example of a later work by the artist using a commercially derived subject that she would repeat many times. (G.N. Hilfiker)

by folk-art historian Harold Pearse, these later works are "consistently and repetitively drawn, and are more likely derived from two-dimensional graphic sources: Christmas cards, postcards and other popular illustrations." The early representations found on the house and the utilitarian objects within it, however, are primarily of flora and fauna brought together in relationships which are Maud's own interpretations of her immediate world: huge butterflies hover over swans of similar size, and tulips of wondrous hues, including bright blue, abound. Only occasionally does a human figure intrude — a jockey astride a speeding horse next to a horse-drawn chariot on the back wall and a silhouetted woman dancing amidst floating coloured balls above a sleeping figure beneath a palm tree on the interior wall to the right of the large window. Clearly these are not everyday scenes from Maud's sequestered life, and most likely, they, too, derive from an external source.

Storm Door

The evolution of the painted design on the storm door took place over a period of approximately ten years. A photograph taken in 1950 by Bert Wetmore of the Halifax *Chronicle Herald* reveals a raw wood surface, devoid of decoration. By 1956, the door had been whitewashed and the central bouquet of flowers with a single yellow butterfly in the upper left had appeared. Maud had added three flying birds in bright primary colours — red, blue, and yellow — by the year 1961 and had developed the bouquet into one fairly overflowing with tulips. The painted storm door attained its final state by 1963, with her addition of three elements to the lower section: a deep blue hummingbird, an orange butterfly at the bottom left, and a black and yellow honeybee to the right, all more or less the same size. The final effect is one which resonates with life and

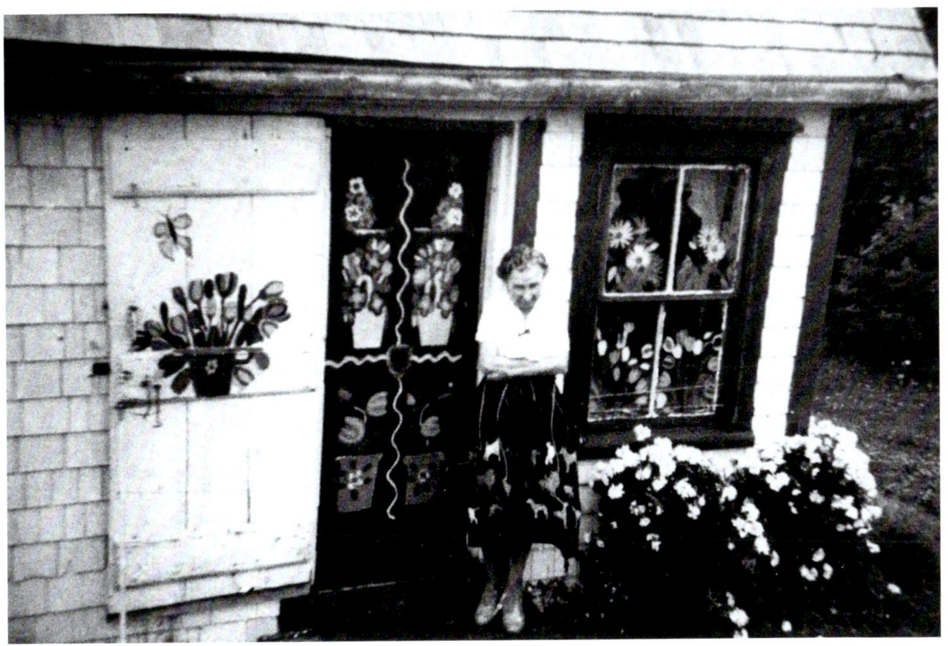

House façade as it appeared in August 1956. Maud had painted the central bouquet and a single butterfly on the storm door at this point.
(Reproduced by Peter Parsons, courtesy of Livia Adalaar)

organic abundance and confirms, without doubt, Maud's innate ability to portray movement and vitality.

Recognizing its commercial potential, a restaurant owner approached Maud with a proposal to hang the door in her establishment as a way to garner interest from tourists. Thus began the period when the house was stripped of this stunning visual element. In its place, Everett hung a second storm door onto which he had painted a small horse beside an evergreen tree — a poor substitute for Maud's bright, eye-catching work. Her storm door eventually resurfaced for sale at a commercial gallery in Halifax. Trimmed at the top and bottom, the door was smaller, but fortunately its main decorative components remained untouched and in remarkably good condi-

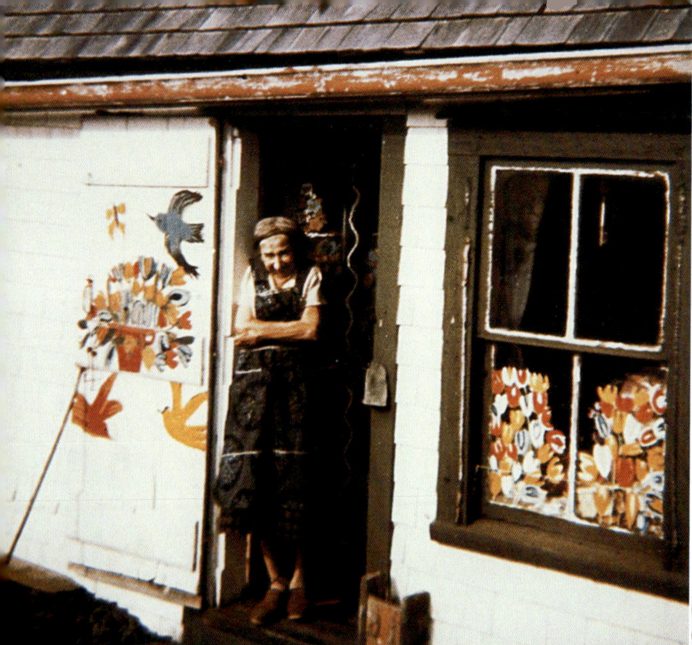

Front façade and Maud in 1961. Note the addition of three flying birds to the storm door. (Cora Greenaway)

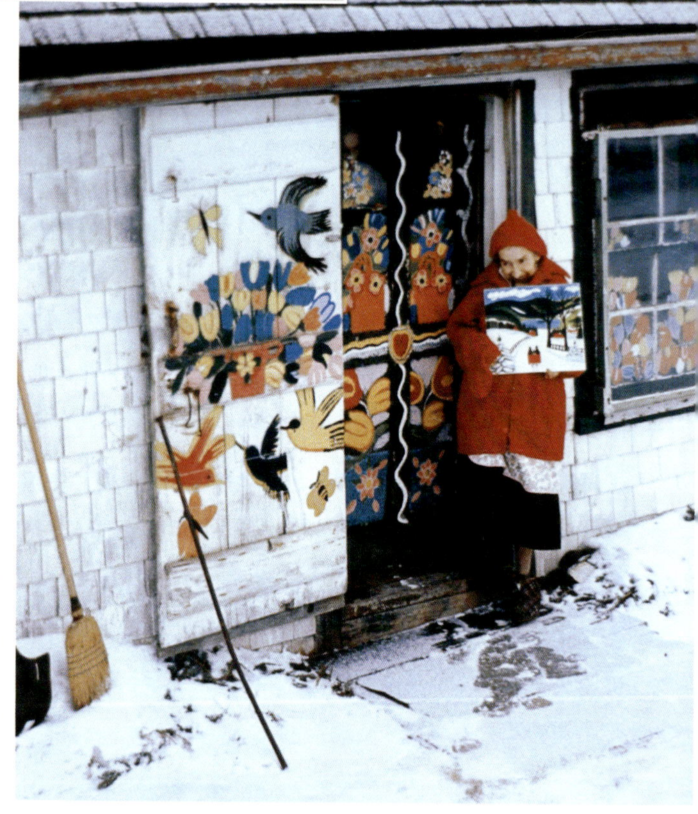

Final state of the storm door as it appeared in 1965. Maud has added three elements to the lower section: a flying bird and two butterflies. (Bob Brooks)

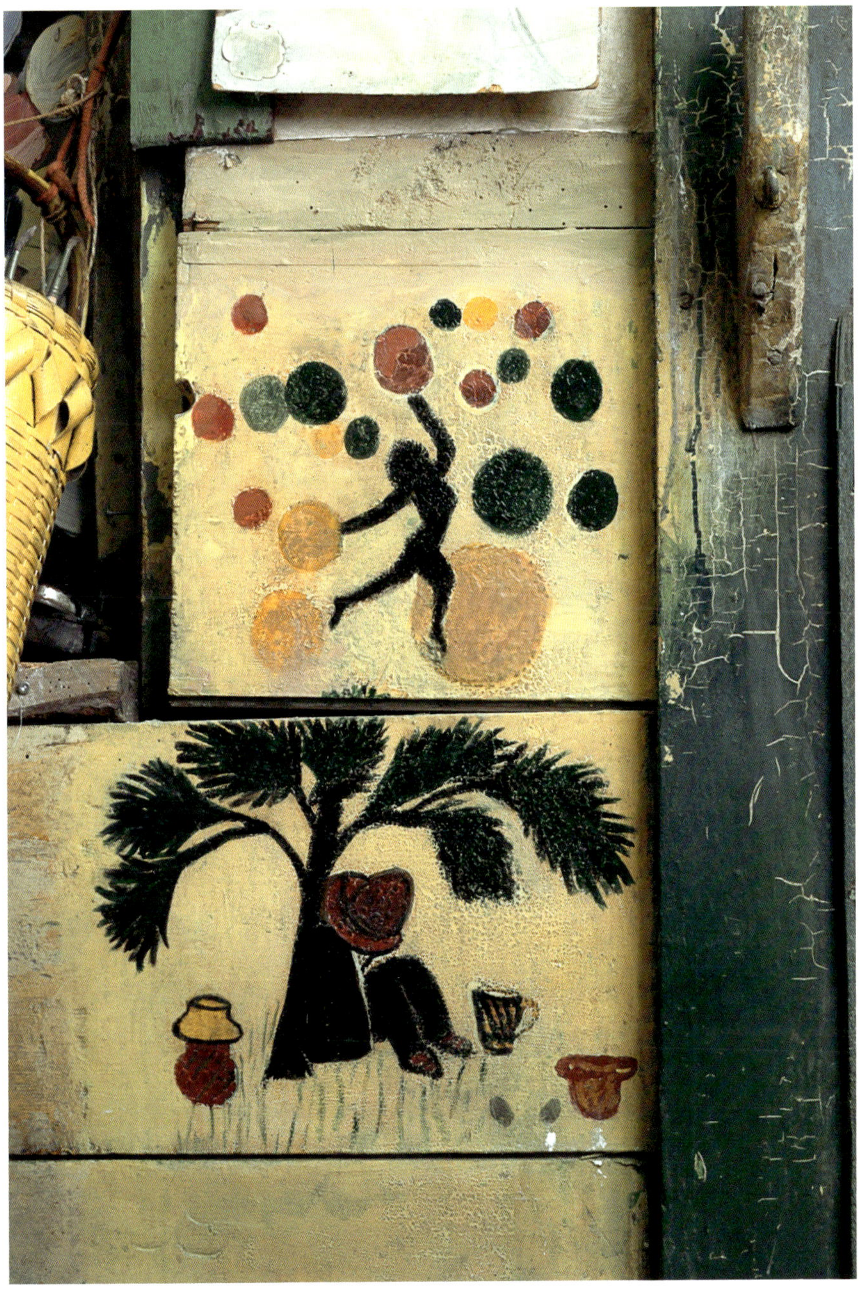

Unusual images found on the south inside wall of the house to the left of the door. (Gary Castle)

tion. Purchased by the Government of Nova Scotia and subsequently restored to its original dimensions, Maud's storm door has, at last, returned to its rightful place at the entrance to her house.

Front Door

The door consists of two small windows placed above four rectangular, recessed panels set into raised cross and side sections (rails and stiles). This structural arrangement forms the basis for the balanced design that Maud would rework but not alter much over the course of her life. Central to her scheme are two sets of symmetrical flower bouquets on the wood panels and floral embellishments on the window panes. In the 1950s, two-handled jugs occupied the top two panels, but by 1956, these were changed to a basket-style design with single curved handles. This was to remain the look of the door until Maud's death in 1970. Serpentine lines adorn the crosspieces and converge at the centre to form a heart-shaped motif; an organically derived ivy vine in silver paint, added later to the stiles, completed the effect.

Unlike the painting on the storm door, which Maud freely developed and added to over time, the design for the exterior of the main front door was fully worked by the 1940s. As years passed, Maud repainted it again and again, so much so that, by the time of her death, the thickness of the paint layers reached about 2 to 3 millimetres (⅛ inch). A small paint sample taken from the top right panel for analysis by cross section photomicrography reveals no less than twenty layers of paint ranging from the blue of the uppermost layers through green, yellow, and blue again near the bottom.

The back of the front door, rarely seen by anyone but the Lewis couple, is a playful attempt by Maud at mirrored symmetry. Using the natural dividing line running down the centre of the door, she repeated the butterflies and black and white swans on each side

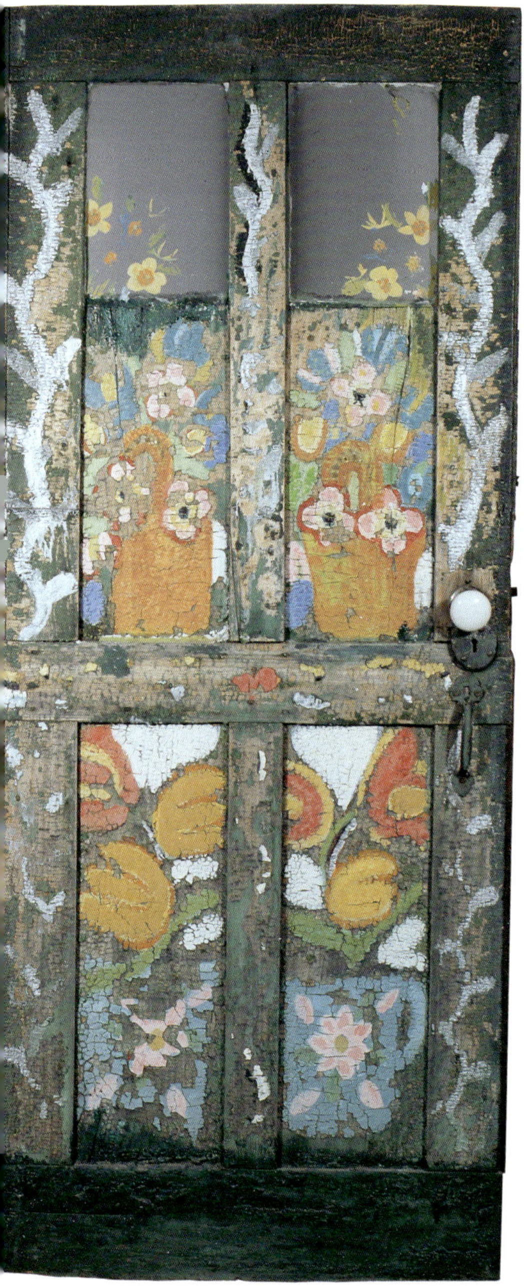

Front panelled door in its present state, showing the weathering and paint loss from years of exposure to the harsh climate. (G.N. Hilfiker)

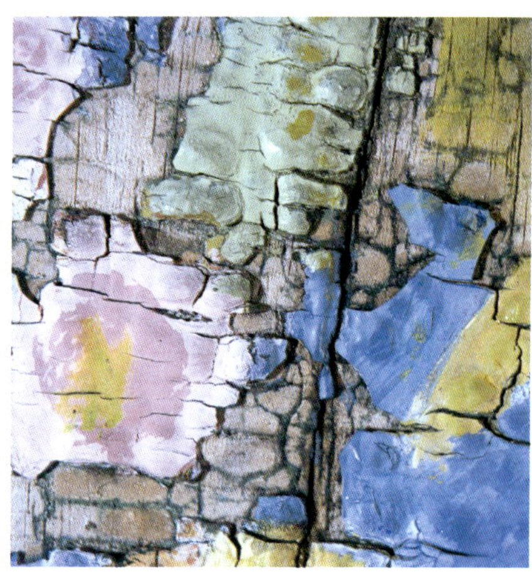

Detail of the front door, revealing the thickness of the paint and the extent of damage and loss. (Laurie Hamilton)

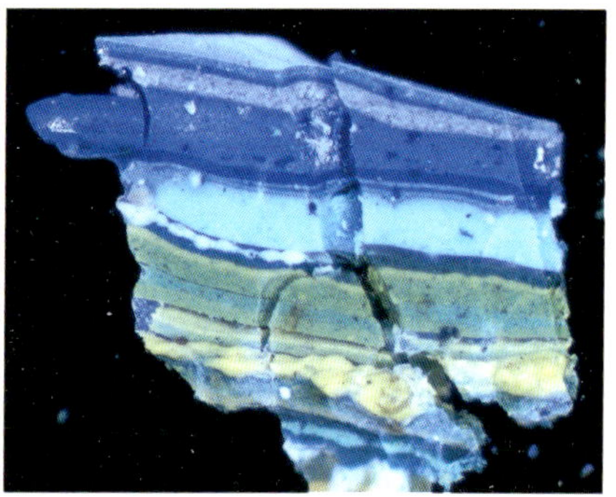

This photomicrograph cross-section of a paint sample taken from the front door reveals no fewer than twenty layers of paint (magnification: 50 x). (Laurie Hamilton)

but with reverse positioning. A single spotted red, yellow, and black butterfly breaks this symmetry. Like the weathered outer surface, where large areas of the thick paint fell prey to the forces of the harsh climate, the inner side reflects a corresponding reality — the intense heat given off by the wood-burning stove. The wide shrinkage cracks now present in the paint film indicate continual heat damage; largely confined to the lower section, the cracks reveal how the door, when swung inward, rested in close proximity to the ferocious heat generated by the firebox.

Front Window

Photographs taken of the front facade over the years document the various decorative incarnations of the four rectangular panes of glass in the large window. Maud had painted the upper two panes early in her married life and had added the treasured tulip imagery to the bottom panes by 1956. It is not surprising that by 1970, only the bottom two panes retained their decoration. Inevitably the victims of breakage, the windows must have been repainted several times throughout Maud's married life. There is an interesting detail about the painted glass decoration: Maud carefully replicated the images on both sides of the glass to ensure that those looking from inside or out would gain the same visual impact.

Interior Decoration

The images Maud favoured for the objects that surrounded her every day of her life reveal the free, unfettered spirit that inhabited her crippled body. Dating from the early part of her career, when she was literally searching for any surface on which to paint — a breadbox, a warming oven, or the papered walls — no object or surface was deemed unacceptable as long as it presented a relatively flat surface.

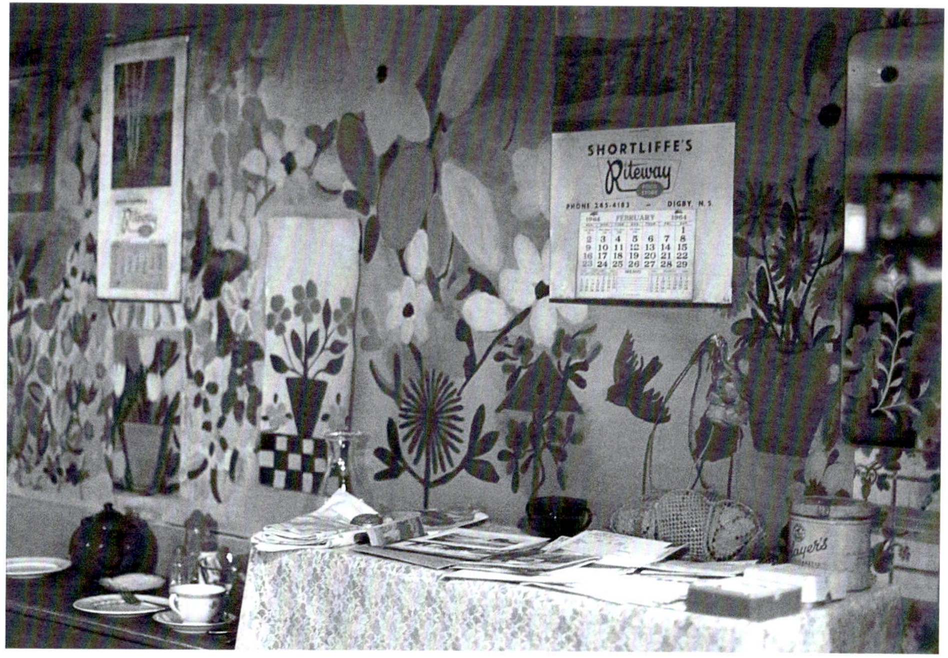

The east wall, with restored wallpaper. (Laurie Hamilton)

The plastered area above the wooden wainscotting on all four walls was covered with paper: a commercial wallpaper with a small-scale abstract pattern in browns and greens covered the front wall and the wall on the left from the front door. An ivy-patterned paper overlaid a small section of the east wall abutting the window, while a monochromatic paper of pale grey-green tone was chosen for the back and right walls. It was on these green walls that Maud let her imagination soar, filling the space with sinewy stems, leaves, and all manner of multicoloured blossoms. Interspersed among the flora are birds and butterflies and occasionally discrete scenes, like a deer among snow-covered trees, all spun around an eclectic assortment of commercial decorative material including calendars, cards, photographs, and wall ornaments.

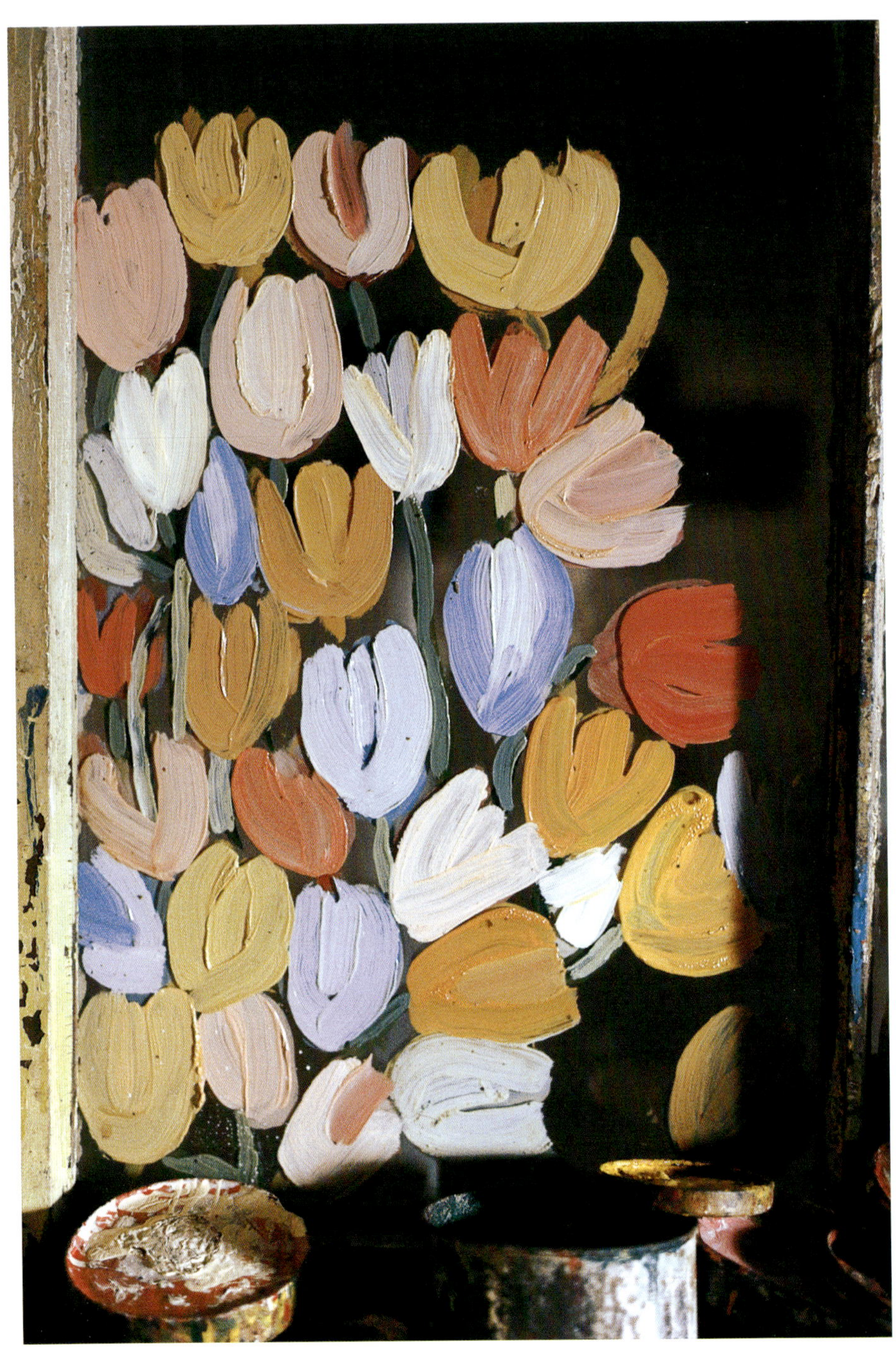

Bottom right interior pane of the window, showing the pristine condition of the painted tulips. (Laurie Hamilton)

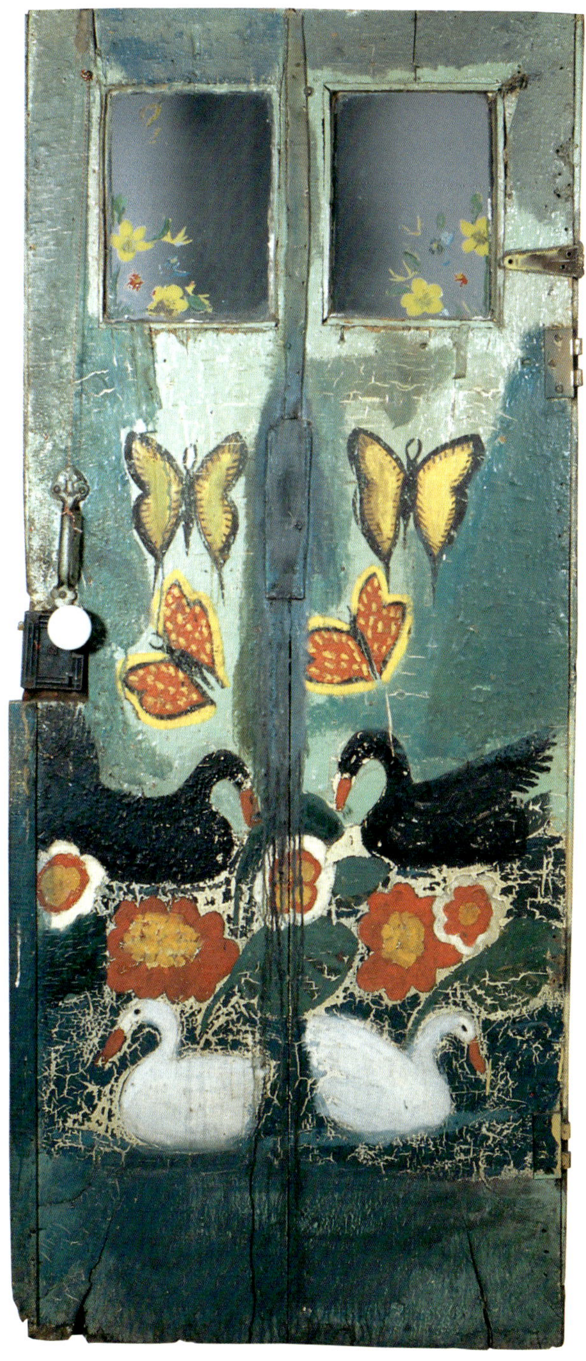

Interior of the front door, illustrating Maud's use of mirror imaging in her design. (AGNS)

Maud also used collage in her interior decorative designs. The old cupboard door at the back right corner features two motifs clipped from magazines — a large black cat (an image which figures prominently in many of Maud's paintings) with a typical family unit of mother, father, and three children and a photograph taken by Bob Brooks of Maud and Everett eating dinner. Beneath these poignant images fly an array of butterflies painted in black and yellow. This collage technique is repeated on the walls where cutouts of monarch butterflies and paper shaped into petals have been glued to the wall surface and integrated into the painted design.

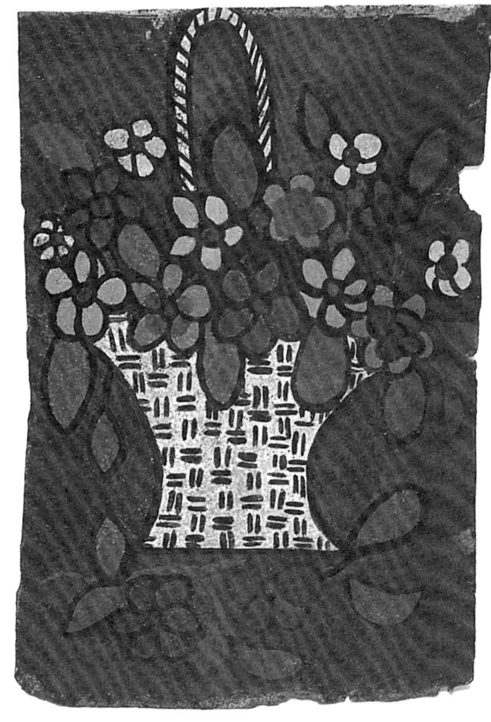

This visually stunning painting of a basket of flowers on a deep crimson background is executed on an irregular scrap of linoleum. (Jennifer McLaughlin)

The many painted utilitarian objects boast an assortment of images, but most prominent are the ubiquitous spring flowers, especially on the metal pieces. Some are simply placed and executed, as those found on the three breadboxes; others are more stunningly representative of Maud's decorative skill, as in the dramatic presentation of red and white flowers on a black tray or the equally attractive tea canister, with its bright orange flowers set against a black grid on a lime green base.

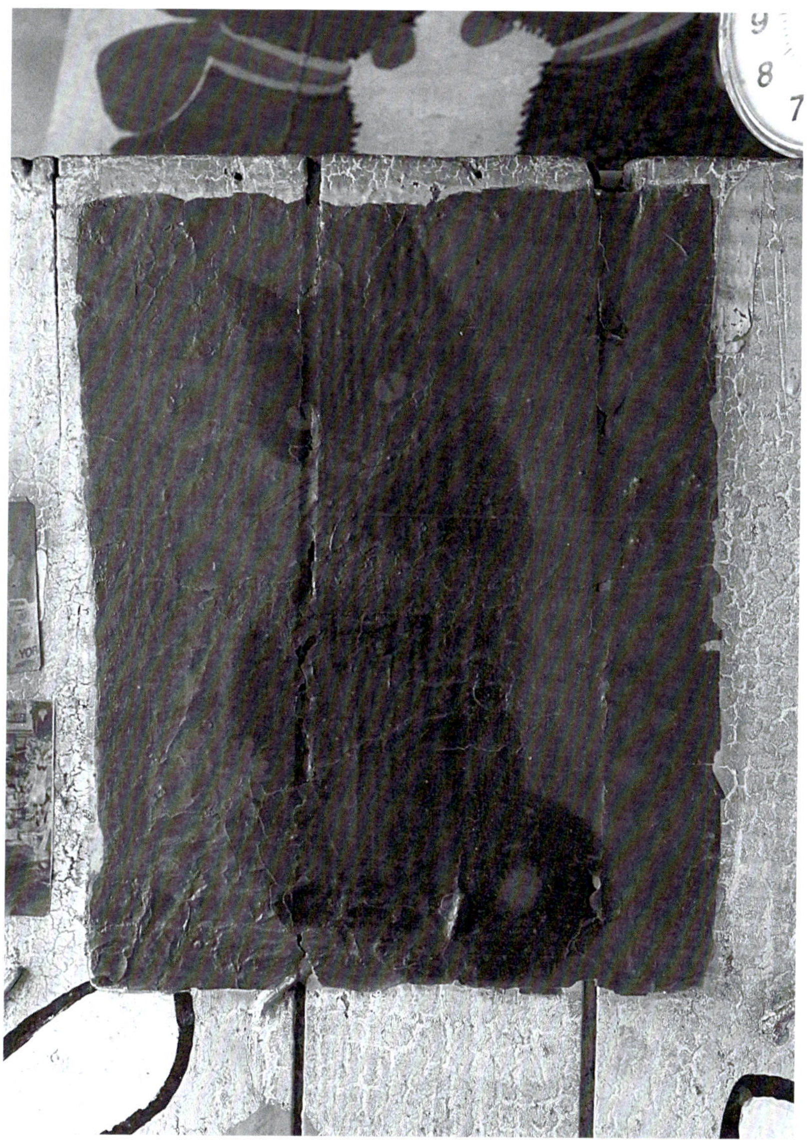

Maud loved cats and painted them many times during her life. This photograph of a black cat glued to the cupboard door likely served as a reference image for many of these paintings. (Gary Castle)

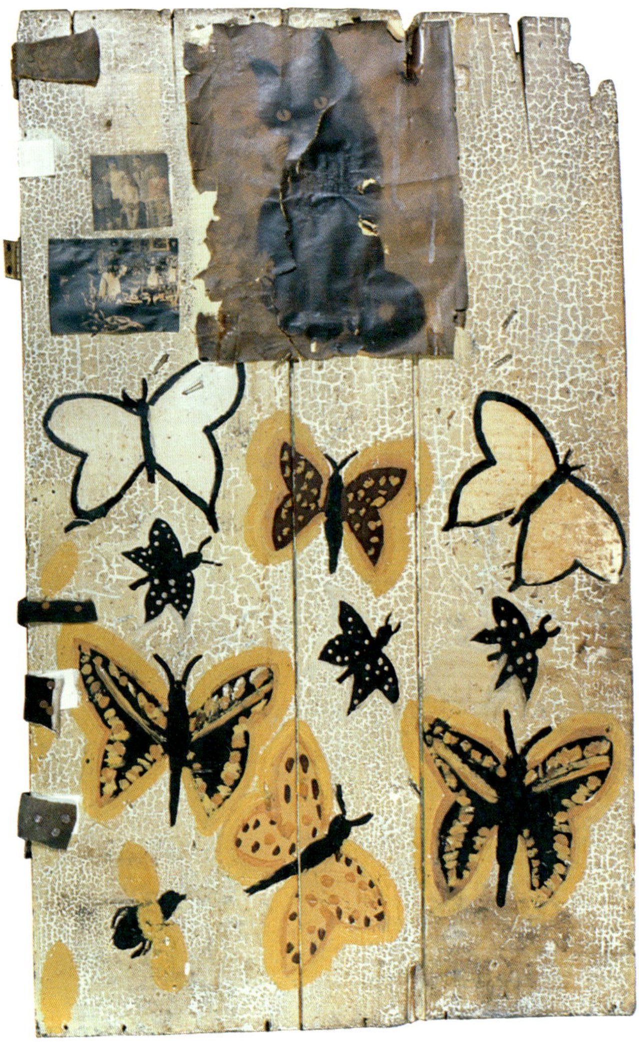

Cupboard door with flying butterflies and cutout images pasted to the surface.
(Laurie Hamilton)

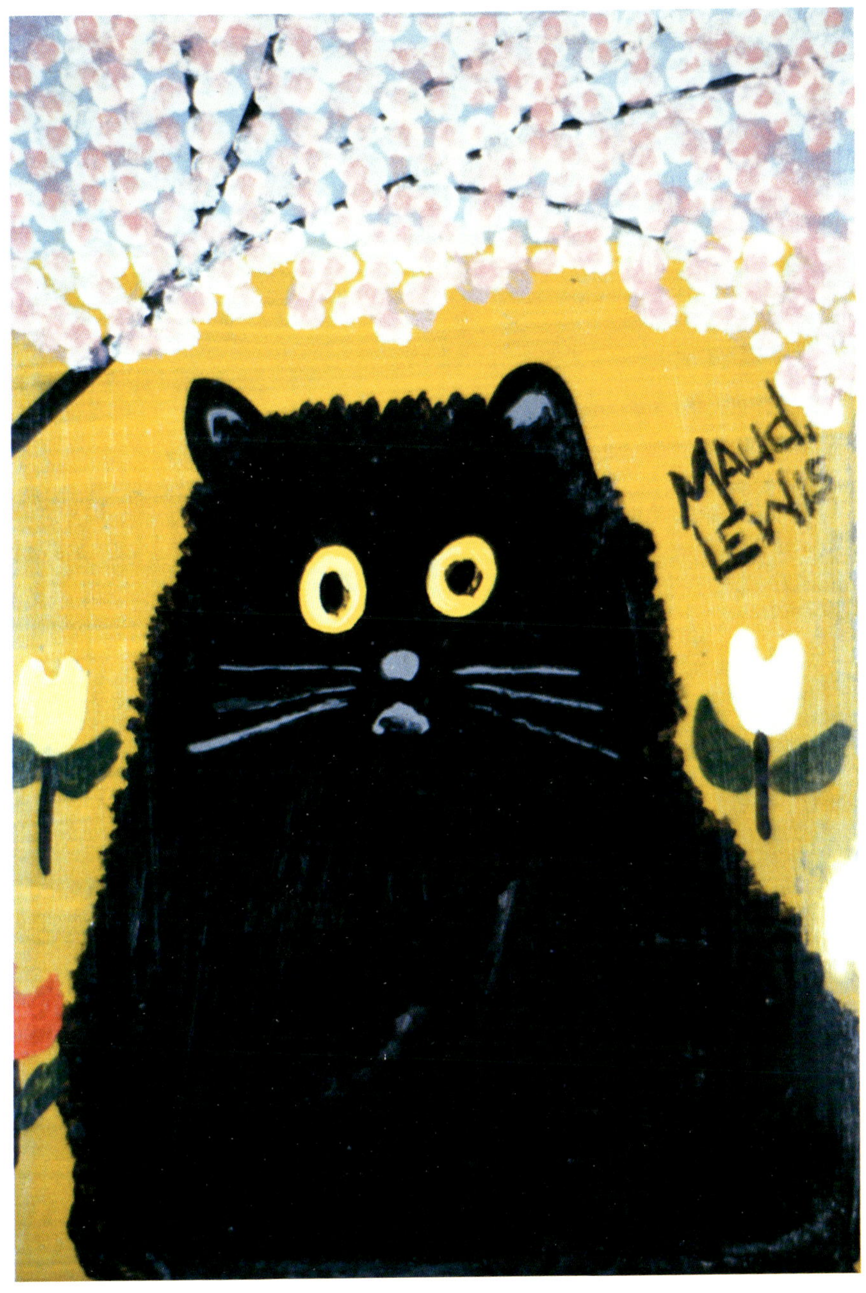

One of Maud's typical paintings of a black cat.
Collection of Pat and Bob Burstall. (Laurie Hamilton)

One cannot help but be moved by the power of these images, juxtaposed against the fragmentary nature of the materials Maud was driven to use as her "canvas." Take, for instance, the scrap of linoleum with its ragged edges, onto which Maud painted a magnificent basket of pink, blue, and yellow flowers against a backdrop of deep crimson red. Here indeed is evidence of one person's need to express and give substance to an inner vision which belies the reality of her impoverished existence.

Curatorial Considerations

Research to establish the validity of the presentation underlies any display. We consulted both oral and archival records to determine the historical accuracy of our presentation. Although many people offered a wealth of wonderful anecdotes about the house and its occupants, it quickly became clear how notoriously unreliable human memory can be, especially for those all-important fine details. People recollected the overall cluttered look inside the house, and many commented on the smell of wood and cigarette smoke combined with paint fumes, but few could pin down the exact location of objects and furnishings. Our search for archival records intensified, honing in particularly on the photographic documentation available from various sources. The classic saying, "a picture is worth a thousand words," proved true again and again as the discovery of an old photograph clarified, in an instant, an area of previous uncertainty. Photographic documentation is one of the cornerstones of modern conservation practice and ensures that those who follow will have the critical visual material essential to making informed decisions. The success of the restoration of the Maud Lewis Painted House rests, in large measure, on those who, for whatever reason, were inspired to take pictures.

Prominent among these was photographer Bob Brooks, sent by the Toronto-based *Star Weekly* in 1965 to record Maud and Everett in their tiny abode for an article with national circulation. These wonderful images, many of which now grace the walls of the Maud

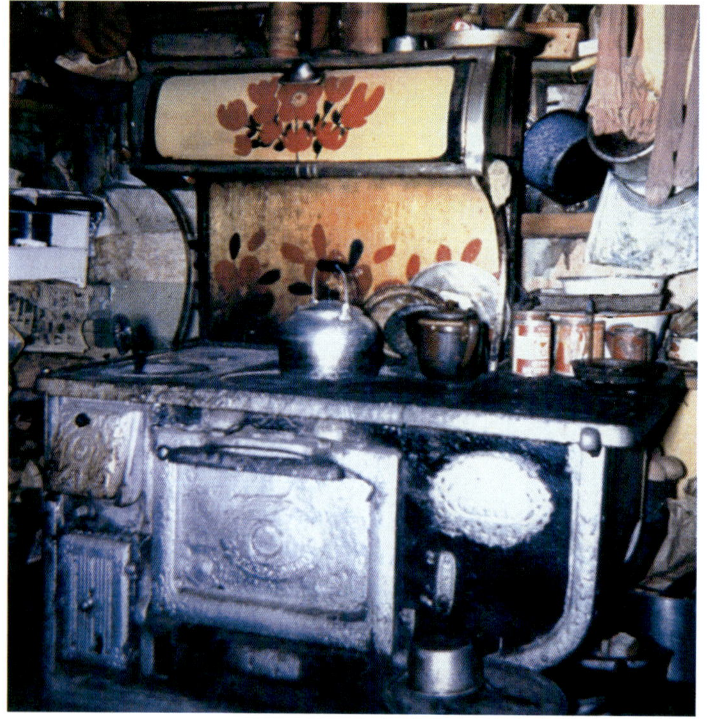

The large cookstove, the focal point of the couple's daily existence, at is appeared in 1966. Archival photographs such as this one were crucial to the restoration project. (Glenn Atchison)

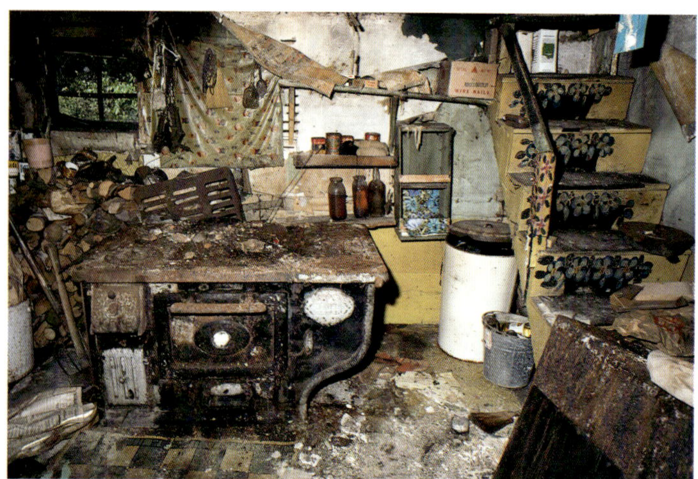

Condition of the stove in the house at its original site in Marshalltown in 1984. (AGNS)

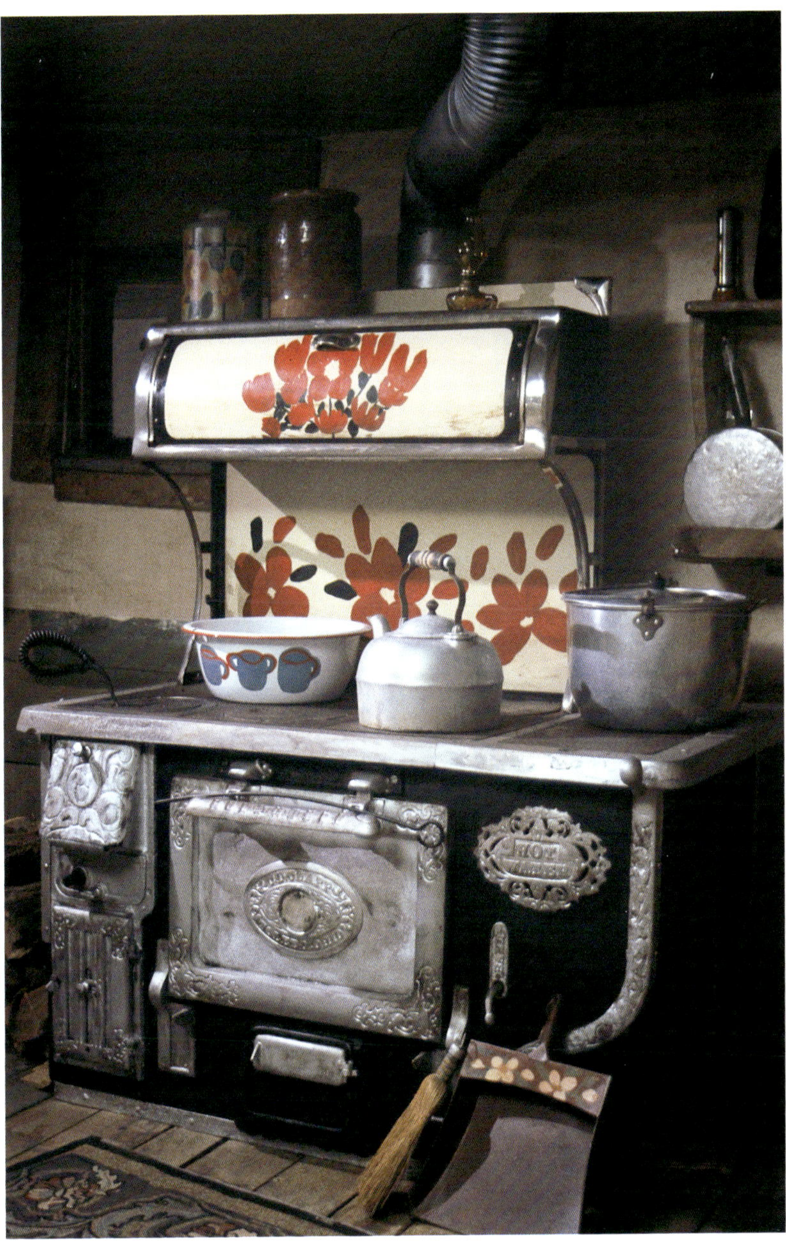

The large cookstove after restoration treatment and re-installation in the restored Maud Lewis Painted House. (Laurie Hamilton)

Lewis gallery, were pivotal for determining the exact placement of objects within the house during the period when Maud was at the height of her commercial success. That same year, the Canadian Broadcasting Corporation aired a half-hour documentary on the Lewis couple, *The Once-Upon-a-Time World of Maud Lewis*, as part of its *Telescope* series, and the CBC generously made a videotape of this documentary available to the AGNS for research purposes. Combined, these two sources established the time-frame to which the interior display would relate and provided a powerful tool which would be utilized throughout the conservation project.

Another set of photographs surfaced from the AGNS registration files, far less refined than the professional work by Brooks but no less crucial for the restoration of the hand-painted wallpaper Maud created on the back and east walls. Half the original paper remained extant, albeit in very poor condition, but the rest had been lost to the ravages of time. Four slide transparencies, taken in poor lighting conditions with a hand-held camera, documented the details of the missing images. Simply put, without these, a full restoration of the wallpaper would not have been possible.

While the interior of the house had not undergone significant changes after Maud's death, the exterior had sustained a number of modifications during Everett's nine-year tenure alone there. Most prominent of these was the addition of evergreen trees, numbering twenty-five in all, randomly painted on the shingles of the front facade. He also decided, for reasons unknown, to paint the naturally weathered roof shingles white on the front slope and red on the back. Everett also added red to some of the wood trim which previously had been green.

What to do about this dilemma? Ethically we could not undo a decade of changes which were as much a part of the house's history as those made during Maud's lifetime. We decided to respect these alterations and restore the house exterior to its 1979 appearance, as at Everett's death, with one exception — the original storm door, brightly painted by Maud, would be returned to the entranceway.

The stove was another difficult artifact to deal with. Crucial to the everyday life of the Lewis couple and formidable in size and presence, it was perhaps the single painted utilitarian object most people recalled as part of the house interior. Unfortunately, it was also in desperate condition: the sheet metal components had rusted beyond repair, although the cast iron sections were deemed salvageable. These were stabilized and remounted to a new metal substrate of the same configuration as the original. A vintage warming oven was found and purchased, the same style and size as the old, onto which the images of its painted red flowers were replicated.

Since there had been no electric lighting in the house during Maud's lifetime, the lighting of the interior space required careful consideration. Taking advantage of the primary view into the house from the front entrance, it seemed logical to make use of the front wall for the installation of adequate track lighting which would be in line with the viewer's gaze and cause the least amount of distraction. Additional track was also inserted into the attic opening, hidden from view but effective for washing the back wall. Our goal was to light the space as unobtrusively as possible without sacrificing the visitor's ability to appreciate the painted objects within.

Finally, the curatorial presentation of the Maud Lewis Painted House in a gallery setting is based on the premise that this is a composite artifact whose various parts, in combination, form a single work of art in its own right. The focus was not to document a particular lifestyle, as might be done in a museum environment, but rather to highlight the paintings of a particular artist in their original context as parts of the exterior and interior of her house. With this in mind, the installation ensures that all the painted images are clearly visible, not marred by the clutter associated with the everyday existence of the couple during their lifetime.

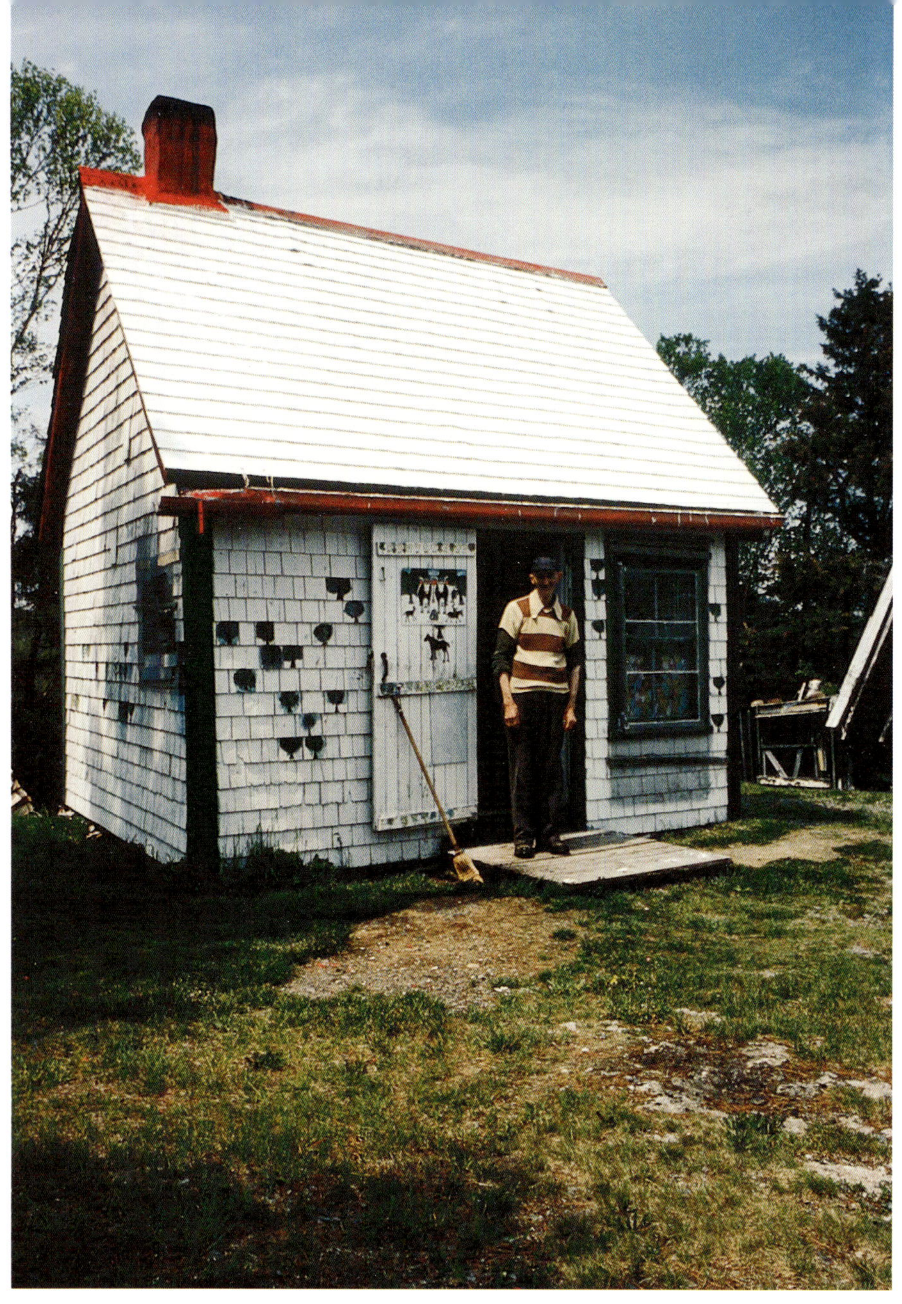

The Maud Lewis Painted House with Everett after Maud's death. Note the freshly painted white roof and the addition of the evergreen trees on the front façade. (Charles Eisener)

Structural Conservation of the House

CRAIG DIX

First Steps

I first saw the Painted House in 1994, at which time I prepared a preliminary report detailing the condition of the house, its treatment needs and their associated costs, including the hiring of a team of three museum-trained technicians to work with me on the project. Once we had the go-ahead, our first concern was to deal with the extensive damage to the house caused by wood-boring insects, especially on the corner boards. Although there was no evidence of current activity, we felt that the building and its contents should be fumigated rather than risk bringing an infestation into the new gallery space. A local pest control company carried out this procedure. The house was tented inside the storage hangar area and treated with methyl bromide gas for twenty-four hours. This chemical is effective and leaves no residue which might harm gallery staff or visitors in future. The hangar was then allowed to vent for two days before we began to dismantle the house.

Dismantling the house

Small as it is, we knew from the outset that the house was too large to be moved into the renovated gallery space in one piece, nor could it be accommodated intact at the Sunnyside Mall conservation site. After consulting with the AGNS construction crew on site, we arranged to bring the house in sections through the oversize opening that would

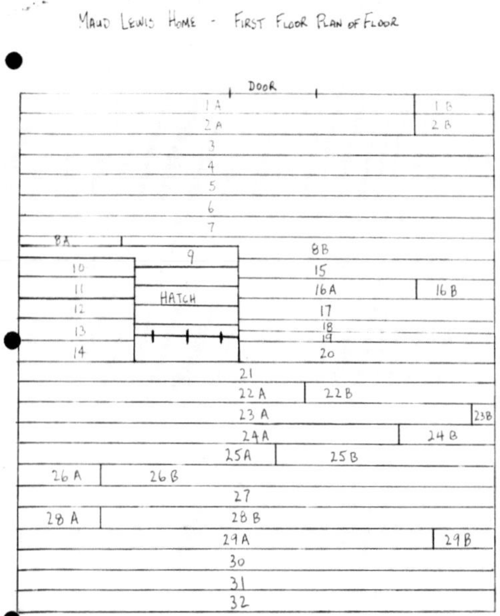

The numbering of the house components and schematic systems for recording data ensured that the house was reassembled exactly as it had been. This diagram shows the sequence of boards for the ground floor. (Laurie Hamilton)

eventually become the main doors to Gallery South of the Art Gallery of Nova Scotia. In order to have the house in sections which were manageable in terms of both weight and size, we decided to remove each side of the roof and the gable end walls in two pieces, cut horizontally, and to leave the front and back walls intact. The deconstruction was guided by two principles: that as little damage be done to the building as possible and that, upon re-assembly, no visible signs remain to reveal that the procedure had ever taken place. To achieve this, we carefully removed a row of shingles from each area where cuts were to be made. Once replaced, the shingles would completely conceal the saw lines.

We established a numbering system for the various components as they were removed to ensure that each would be returned to its original position. The rows of shingles, the corner boards, ridge cap, floorboards for the first and second floors, and floor joists for the second floor each received a number.

After removing the contents of the house, we took off the corner boards, ridge cap, soffits, and fascia boards in preparation for dismantling the roof. The nails were cut along the ridge of the roof

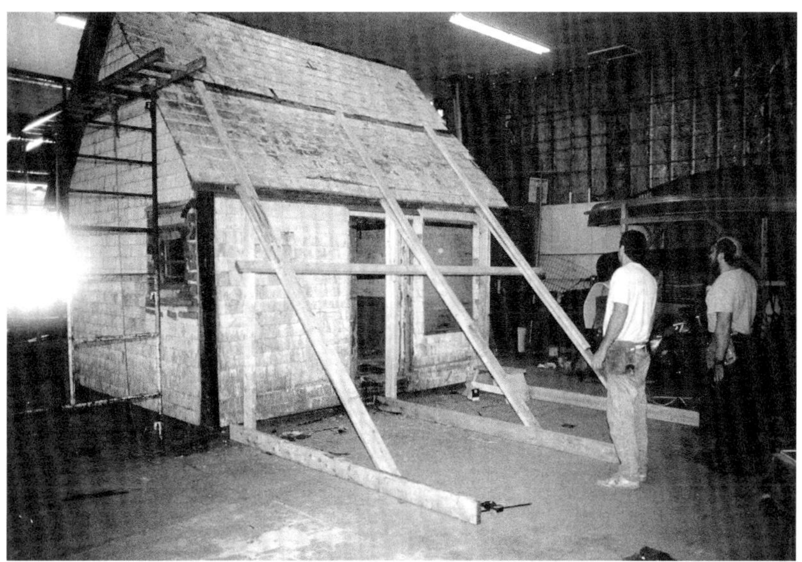

A wooden support mechanism, pitched at the same slope as the roof, supported the considerable weight of the roof sections as they were lowered. (Craig Dix)

to separate the two sides. We then removed a row of shingles at the midpoint of each roof side and cut through the sheathing and rafters horizontally to form two equal parts.

Each roof section was readied to slide down to a frame built at floor level with the same pitch as the roof. Lengths of two-by-four lumber attached to the rear side of each roof section provided additional strength and prevented its racking or twisting upon removal. The top section was then completely detached by cutting through all nails, and the freed section was lowered using ropes tied to the two-by-four on its back. Each section was dealt with in this manner. On the two gable-end walls, we removed a row of shingles at the height of the second floor. These walls were cut in two horizontally and removed in the same manner as the roof.

The next stage was to dispose of the deteriorated ceiling plaster,

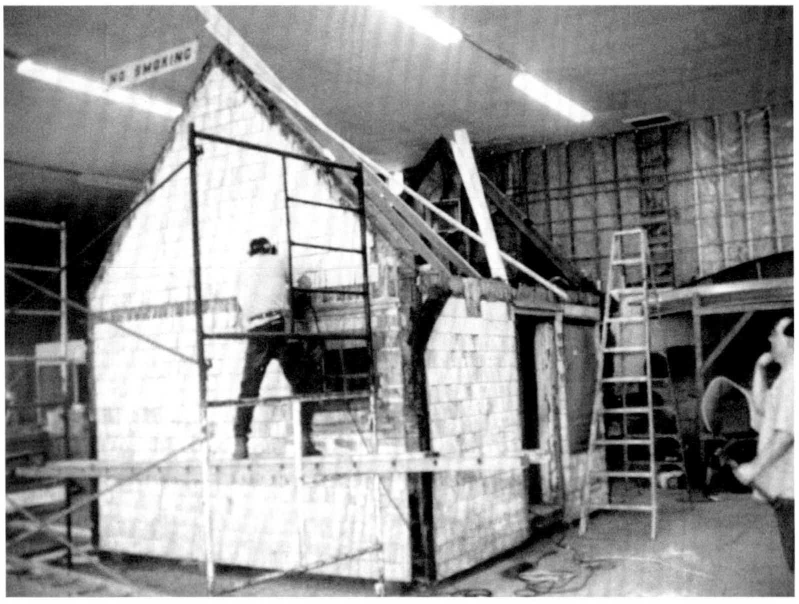

A single row of shingles was removed in order to separate the gable portion of the house. (Bernard Riordon)

which allowed us to remove the second floor beams and joists. Plaster samples from the ceiling were taken for use in colour matching and texturing during the reconstruction phase. Measurements were also taken of shadow lines on the walls which indicated where shelves had been hung in the past. The plaster and lath, as well as the strapping affixed to the underside of the floor joists, were then removed. Once all the elements had been numbered, we dismantled the first and second floors, leaving only the four exterior walls standing.

The nails holding the house together at the corners were cut and the corners temporarily tacked with screws. Since the plaster on the walls was extremely fragile, we tacked sheets of 6mm (¼ inch) fluted plastic, known as Coroplast, in place to minimize plaster loss.

Interestingly, once we were able to see the internal structure of the house, we realized it had been built from the recycled parts of an

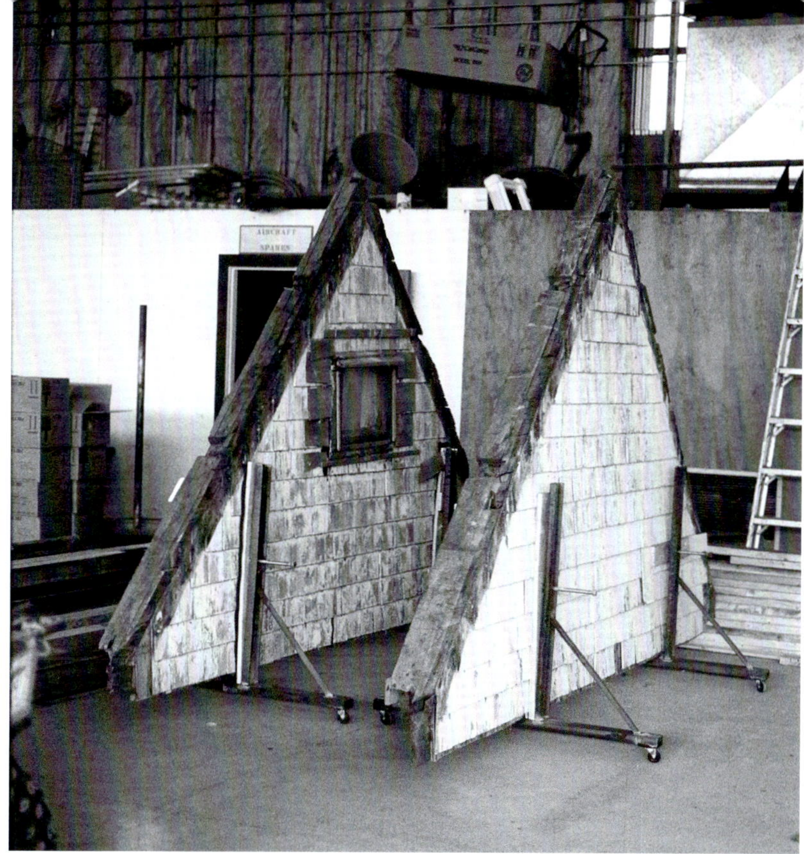

Custom designed T-shaped iron supports on wheels held the ten large sections of the house in an upright position. Without them, moving and storage of the units would have been extremely difficult. (Laurie Hamilton)

earlier building. There were mortise-and-tenon joints on wooden elements that did not connect to anything but were simply being re-used as sound timber.

Moving the House Sections

In a brainstorming session with the crew, we came up with a custom design for a T-shaped iron support system which could be welded together and affixed with casters for manoeuvring. Each support would be made to act like a giant clamp, with a threaded rod to hold the sections gently and safely in an upright position. We built

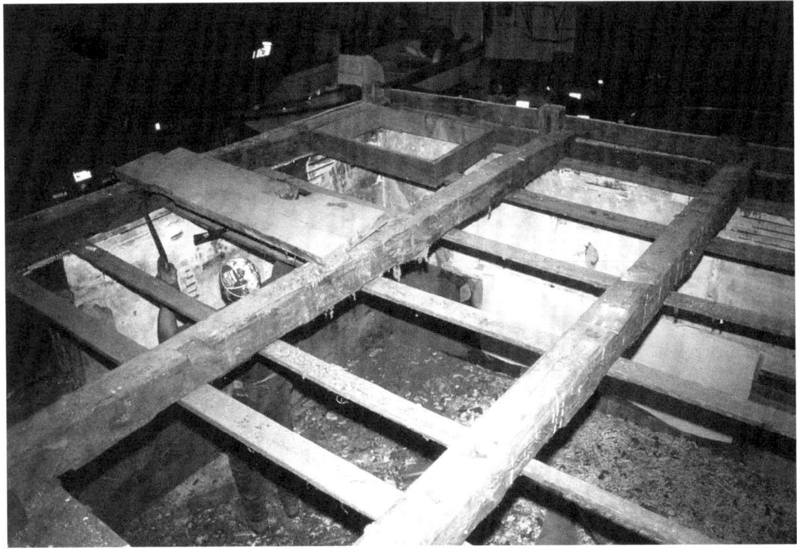

Disassembly stage, showing the beams of the second floor exposed after the removal of the first floor ceiling plaster and the attic floorboards. (Craig Dix)

twenty of these units and placed one at each end of the ten sections. They made moving and transport relatively easy as well as providing an efficient way to store the pieces.

To protect the plaster walls and painted wooden wainscotting, each of the house sections was sandwiched between sheets of Coroplast. A length of two-by-four placed against each structural member protected the fragile surfaces of the house from the damage the threaded rod could potentially have caused. As well, where the weight of the wall rested on a support, we placed a cushion of polyethylene foam, called Ethafoam, for additional protection.

Unavoidable Losses to the Structure

We consulted regularly with AGNS Director Bernard Riordon and Conservator Laurie Hamilton throughout the dismantling and re-assembly operations to ensure all appropriate measures were taken to save as much of the structure as was feasible. The ceiling plaster was in very poor condition, and it, as well as the ceiling lath, had to be removed to disassemble the floor joists of the second floor. The sub-floor on the main level was also extremely degraded. Realizing that gallery staff would need to enter the building on a regular basis to carry out maintenance procedures, the safety of the floor was a real issue. We installed a new sub-floor of decking which gave the floor the same elevation as it had enjoyed initially. The original floor boards would be re-laid over this new material. For visitors to the Maud Lewis House, the visual effect of the interior would remain unchanged.

In spite of our strenuous effort to preserve what remained of the original plaster on the walls, by the time of reconstruction, we realized its condition was too poor for us to salvage it. Like the ceiling, it had no painted decoration and would eventually be concealed by wallpaper anyway, so we decided to remove the old plaster completely but to retain the still-usable underlying original lath.

Sections of the corner boards were rotten or missing altogether, particularly where they had been in contact with the ground or attacked by insects. Rather than replace an entire board, we consolidated the weak areas with a water-based epoxy proprietary product called Petrified Wood, and scarfed on new pine boards to re-establish the correct length and appearance.

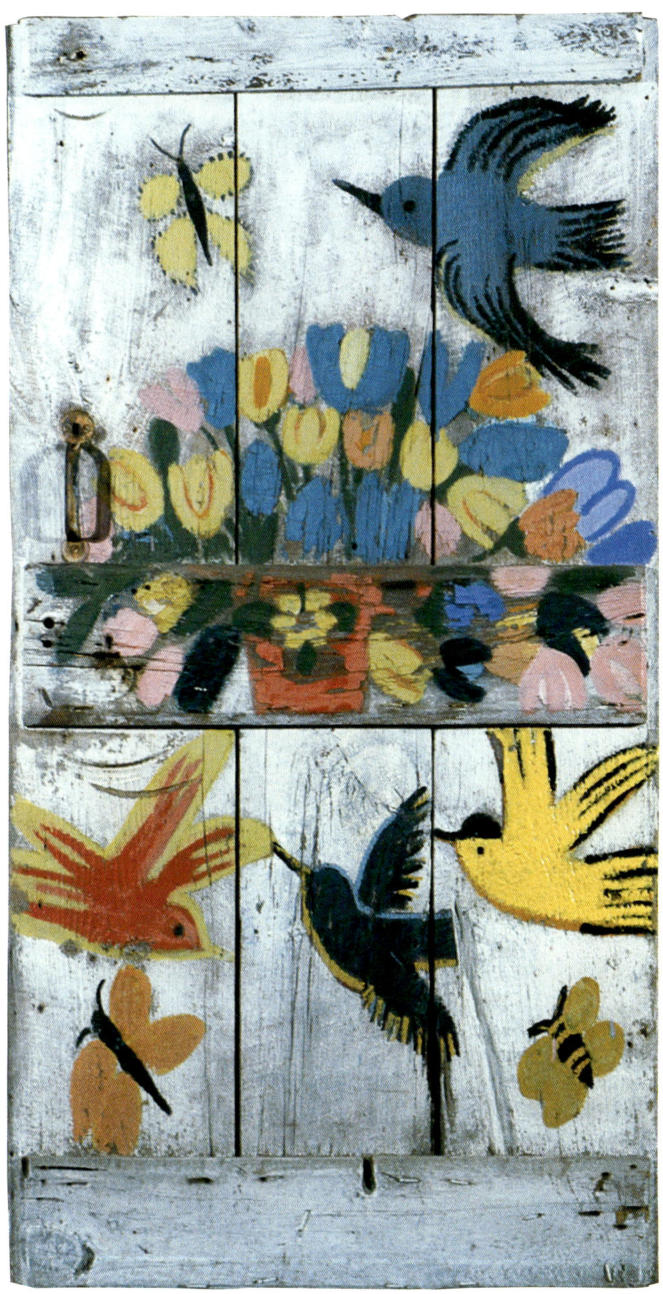

At some point, while the storm door was in private hands, the top and bottom were trimmed through the horizontal battens to reduce the overall height by 35 cm (13¾ inches). Fortunately, Maud's lively images were not affected. (Laurie Hamilton)

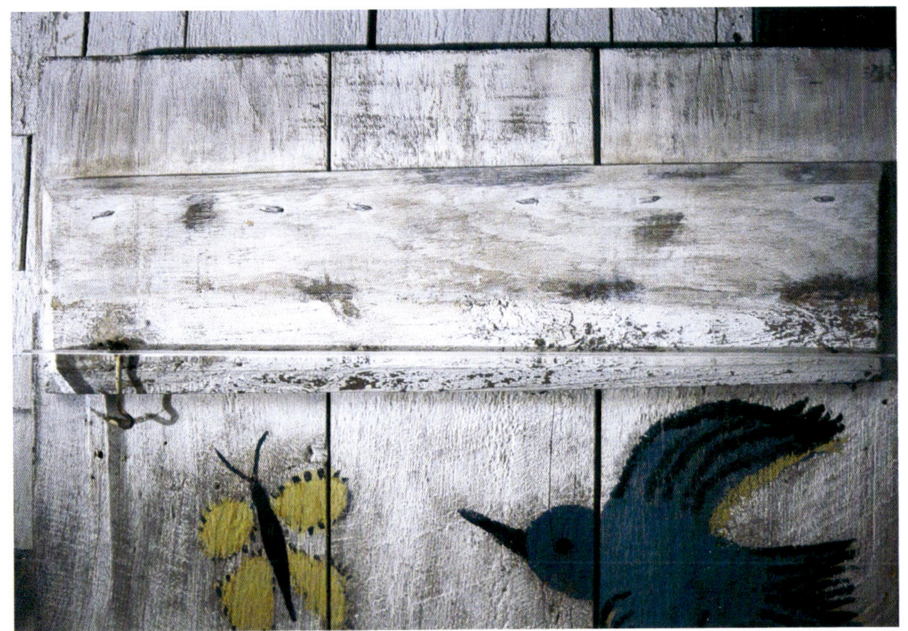

To restore the storm door to its proper dimensions, new wood was added to the top and bottom of the door. This detail shows how appropriate toning of the new wood was completed to blend with the old. (Laurie Hamilton)

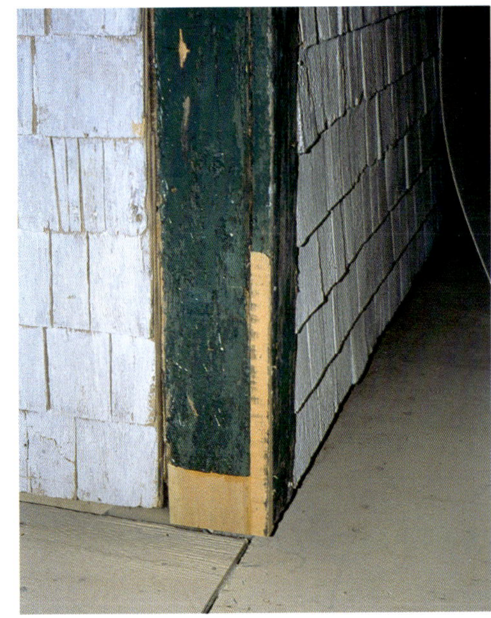

New wood was substituted where rot or insect attack had caused excessive damage to the old. Here a section of the corner board has been replaced prior to painting with the appropriate trim colour. (Kim Jarrett)

Under the Public Eye

The Maud Lewis House was kept in an empty store at Sunnyside Mall, Bedford, while construction on the new gallery progressed. At the Sunnyside location, conservation work continued on the deteriorated front window frame and the beautifully painted stairs. Members of the public were able to speak with both Jennifer McLaughlin, Fine Art Conservator, and myself about the conservation processes. Many also came to share stories about Maud and the legacy of her work. Certainly, the public venue raised awareness about this particular project and brought the conservation profession out from behind the closed doors where we normally operate. The House attracted quite a bit of media coverage during the time we worked on it at the mall. Education is a key element in alerting people to the need to preserve our cultural heritage, and this project was a unique way to reach out to the public and excite their interest in our work.

Front Window and Storm Door Treatment

The front window, one of only three in the house, is a focal point of the building, with brightly coloured flowers painted on both the inside and outside surfaces. Although the panes of glass were in excellent condition, the wood sill was severely deteriorated at one bottom corner, where a large amount of wood was missing. The other corner had also lost a small amount of wood from the tenon. In general, the wood framing was soft from rot.

We used Cold Cure 2 Part Epoxy Resin to consolidate the wood around the missing areas. We employed the same two-part system mixed with a bulking material, Cabosil Fumed Silica, to recreate the lost areas, which were then shaped and textured to resemble a naturally weathered surface. The fill material was painted the appropriate colour during the final touch-up of the house trim.

The storm door is a typical board-and-batten design, consisting of three vertical tongue-in-groove boards held together by three horizontal boards nailed to the back side. Someone in the past had cut through the upper batten and the lower edge of the bottom batten; fortunately, none of Maud's painted design had been lost. Based on an archival photo of the door, we calculated that approximately 18 centimetres (7 inches) had been removed from the top and 12 centimetres (4¾ inches) from the bottom. To extend the vertical boards at top and bottom, we added new pieces of pine, which were dowelled into the originals and adhered with a reversible fish glue. We also added new wood to recreate the width of the battens and restore the door to its original size. The new wood elements were then hand-planed to match the look of the original. As the bare wood would show through in some areas, we patinated the new wood with acrylic paints and used a wire brush to weather the surface of the new wood. The white and green top coats of paint were blended to match the original colours.

Challenges of the Re-Assembly

For the disassembly process at the hangar, we had gravity working in our favour. During the re-assembly at the gallery, however, gravity worked against us constantly as we shifted the large, heavy sections of the house into place. Putting the main walls back up was not too difficult, as they could be muscled into place. We started with the back wall, then tacked on the two side walls temporarily. We reconstructed the house on a foundation of doubled two-by-fours to raise it to the level requested for the new gallery's hardwood flooring, which would be installed at a later date in the surrounding space.

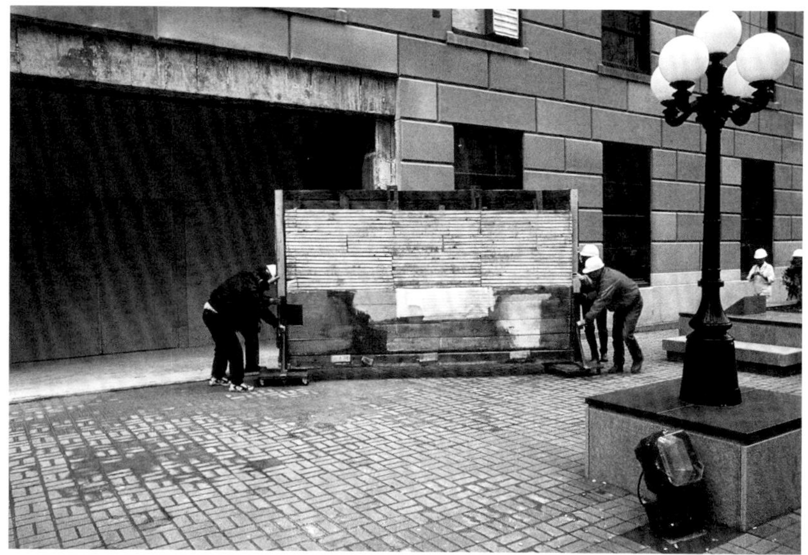

The newly made opening to what would become Gallery South of the Art Gallery of Nova Scotia provided the window of opportunity for moving the large sections of the House into the new gallery space. (Laurie Hamilton)

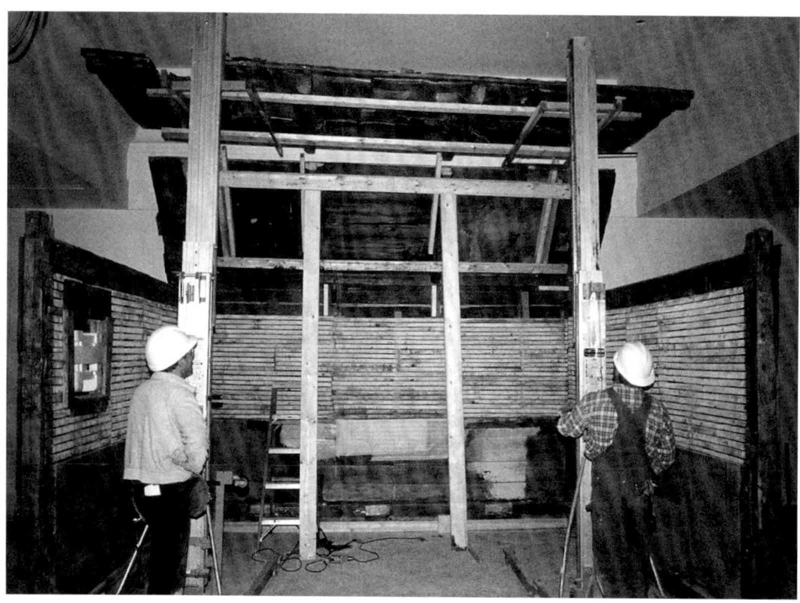

Two hand-hoists used for the installation of drywall proved ideal for gently lifting the roof sections of the House into place. (Laurie Hamilton)

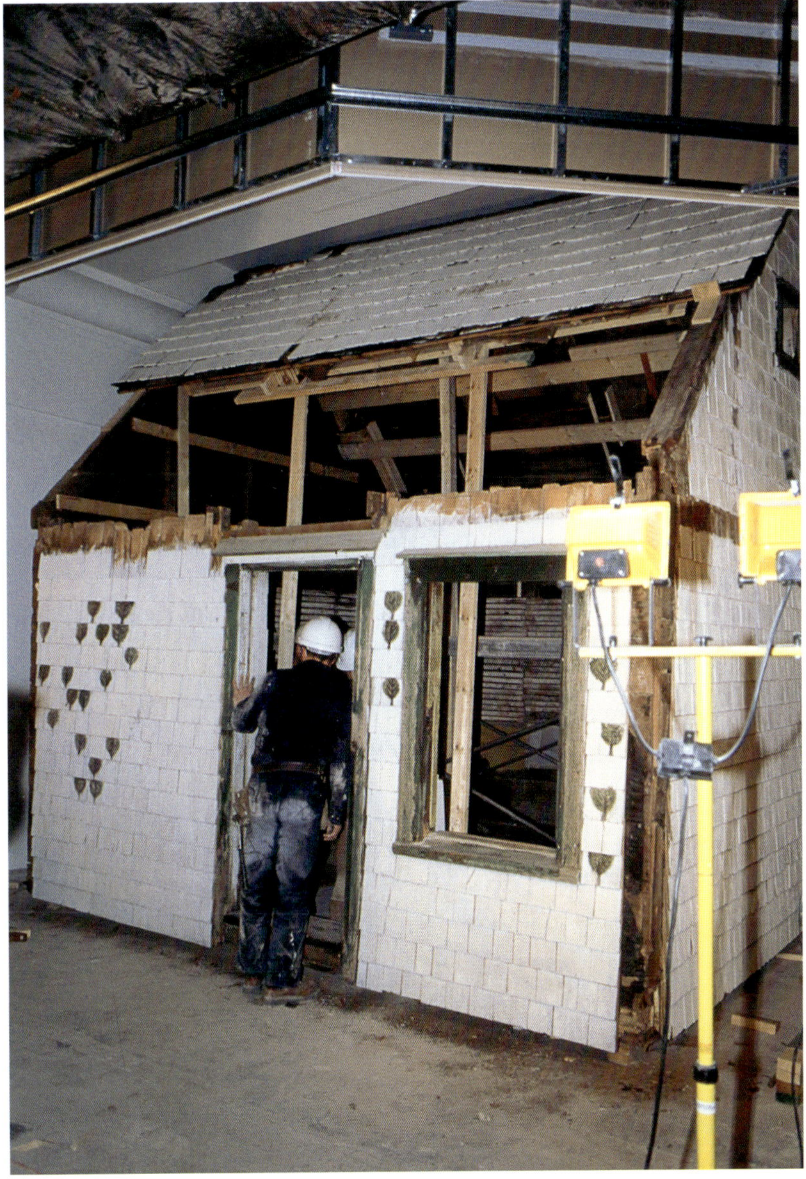

Re-assembly, with nine of the ten sections back in position. (Laurie Hamilton)

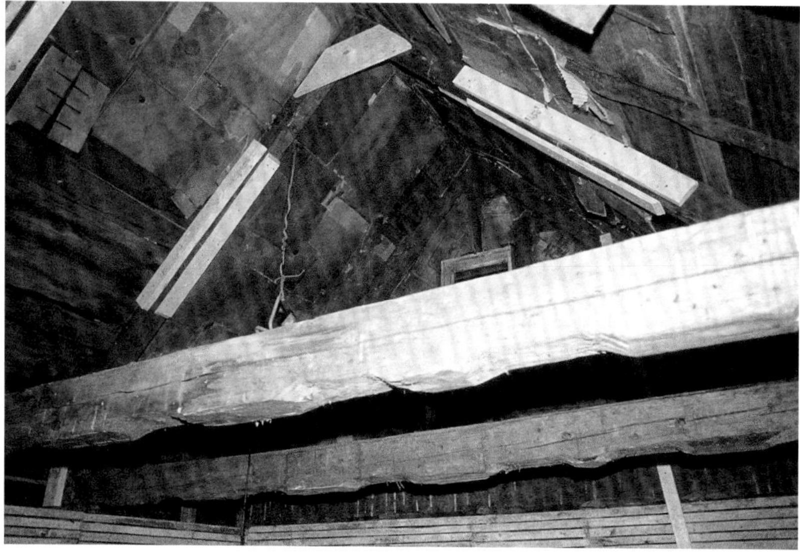

Triangular gussets and lengths of two-by-four were used to re-attach sections of the House which had been cut during the disassembly process. (Craig Dix)

Working alongside the contractors involved in the gallery renovation, we immediately recognized the usefulness of the hand-hoists the drywallers used to lift sheets of drywall up to the ceiling. These hoists (generously made available to us) proved invaluable as a means of elevating the heavy roof sections in a controlled manner to their approximate position, where we could lift them off by hand.

Once settled in position, the bottom portion of the rear roof was braced from below at a slightly steeper pitch than normal. The upper rear portion was then lowered in place and braced, also slightly higher, which enabled the gable ends to be inserted easily into their proper position and attached. The rear roof sections were then lowered and attached with screws. After securing the upper section of the front roof, we fitted the front wall of the house into place. The

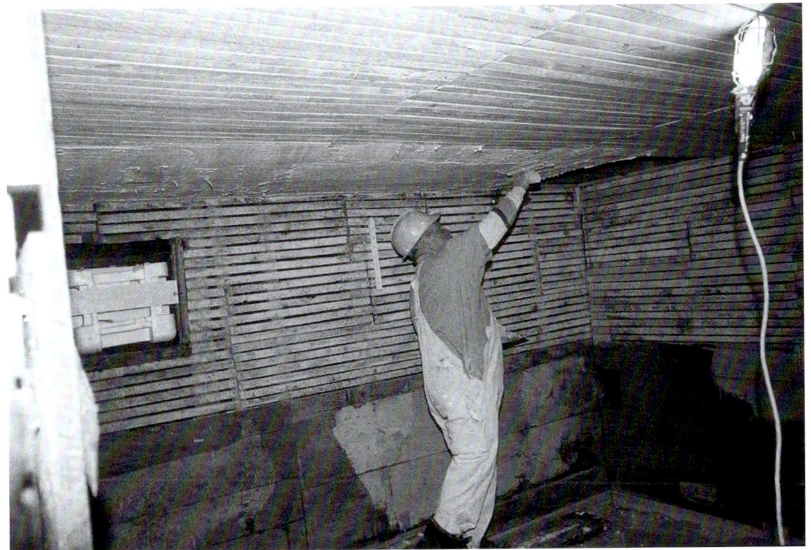

Plasterer Manny MacPherson applies the initial scratch coat to the ceiling lath. (Laurie Hamilton)

final front section of the roof completed the reunification of all ten sections of the house.

Once we had all the major pieces in alignment, we were able to nail the corners of the four walls permanently into the frame. Each roof rafter, which had been cut to disassemble the house, was strengthened with two-by-four lumber and gussets attached under the ridge of the roof. Metal plates tied the gables to the walls and ensured no future movement. Next we re-installed the heavy beams which support the second floor. As the second floor had always been under-built, we added a layer of tongue-and-groove plywood as a safety measure before relaying the old floor. Using our numbered plan, we laid the original floorboards sequentially over this plywood, without nails, just as we had found them.

To strengthen the main floor, we installed two-by-six floor joists under the new sub-floor. Using the numbered plan we had drawn up earlier, we were able to re-install the floorboards in their original positions.

We put the old strapping back in position on the underside of the large beams and applied new ceiling lath in preparation for plastering. An electrician then wired the house with tracks to accept the display lighting. The inside window trim around the small window was removed temporarily to prevent damage during plastering. The plasterer applied a traditional scratch coat and a finish coat of lime plaster, taking care to approximate the less-than-perfect job which had been carried out originally. A week later, we painted the finish plaster with an alkyd primer. To achieve a more authentic look, the ceiling was painted with a brush rather than a roller, using a green latex that matched the original ceiling colour.

The rows of shingles on the ends and roof of the house, which had been removed and numbered before cutting the house into sections, were replaced in their original positions. The wooden eavestroughing along the front of the house, which appeared in the documentary photographs, had been lost prior to its accession by the AGNS. To be faithful to the look and history of the house, a section of old wooden eavestroughing was purchased, installed, and painted red to match archival photographs.

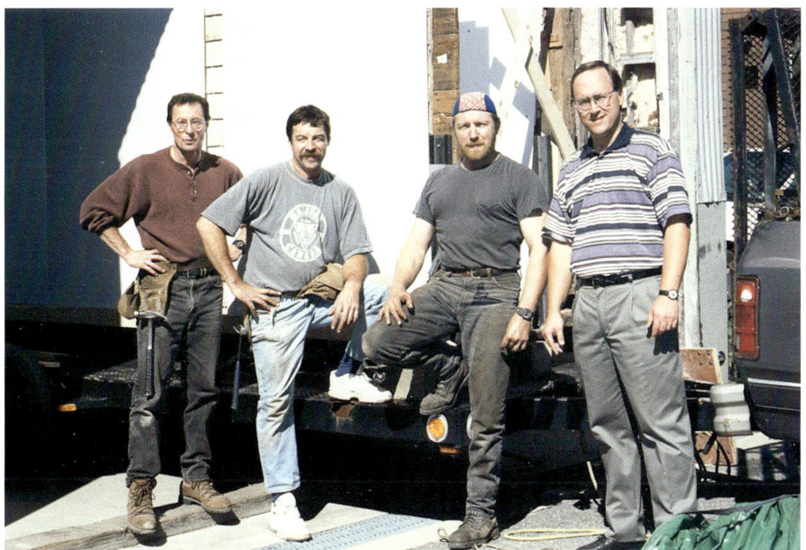

The hard-working team, from left to right: Kim Jarrett, Steve Shannon, Todd Vassallo and Craig Dix. (Laurie Hamilton)

The Team

A great team of three professionally trained museum technicians: Kim Jarrett, Steve Shannon, and Todd Vassallo along with conservator Craig Dix. Their combined expertise and problem-solving capabilities made this stage of the project a success.

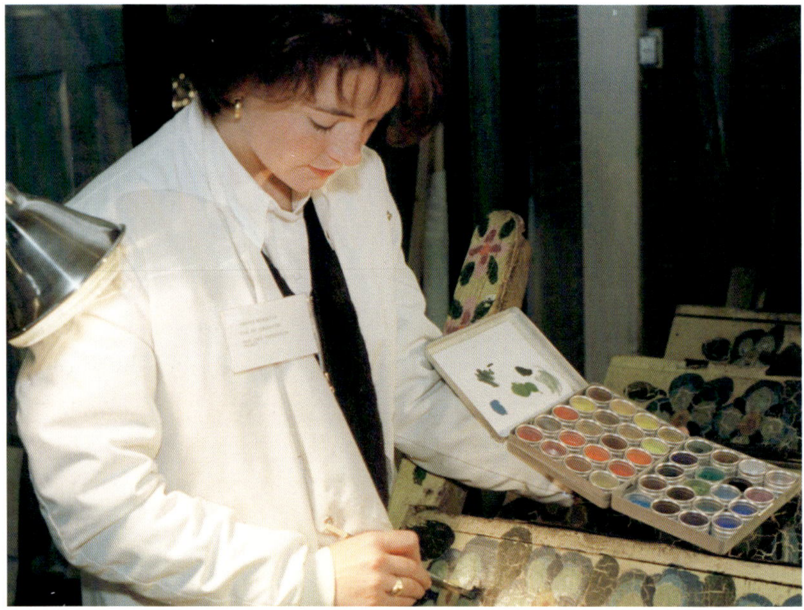

Jennifer McLaughlin working on the staircase in public view at Sunnyside Mall in Bedford, Nova Scotia. (Ryan Van Horne, Halifax *Daily News*)

Conservation of Painted Artifacts

JENNIFER McLAUGHLIN

Maud Lewis's joyous vision of a better reality allowed her to transform her meagre environment into a garden overflowing with bounty by touching every available surface with her magical paintbrush. Some of the most singular and interesting pieces that Maud decorated were functional household objects made from metal: breadboxes, storage tins, serving trays, even a dustpan. Maud painted them all using a combination of low gloss industrial alkyd and oil paints, usually applying her own special choice of background colour over the original manufacturer's colour as a first step. She then decorated the containers with floral designs in bright, contrasting colours.

Three-Dimensional Objects

Lacking electric refrigeration, the Lewises used metal breadboxes for food storage: three traditionally styled breadboxes with sliding doors, as well as one large metal chest with a lid. All four containers were painted a cheerful yellow embellished with red floral designs, mostly of roses and daisies. Interspersed among the painted flowers were small floral decals Maud had applied as a finishing touch.

The paint was generally well adhered to the metal substrate, but an insidious agent of deterioration had been at work. All the metal containers were constructed from thin sheets of tin-plated iron alloy. A layer of orange corrosion product (rust) of varying thickness covered

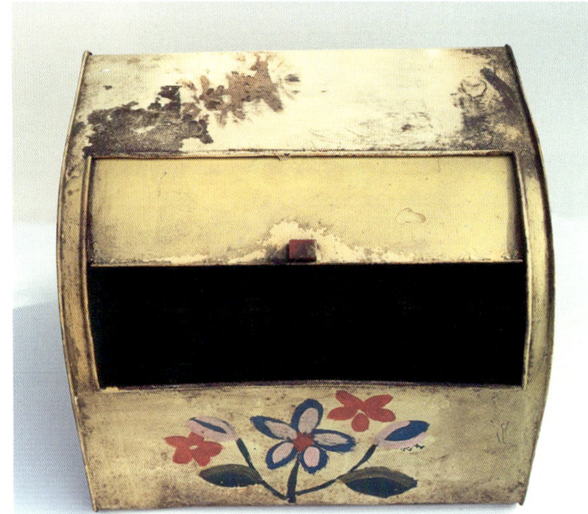

A typical old-style breadbox with a single sliding door, in its before-treatment condition. (Jennifer McLaughlin)

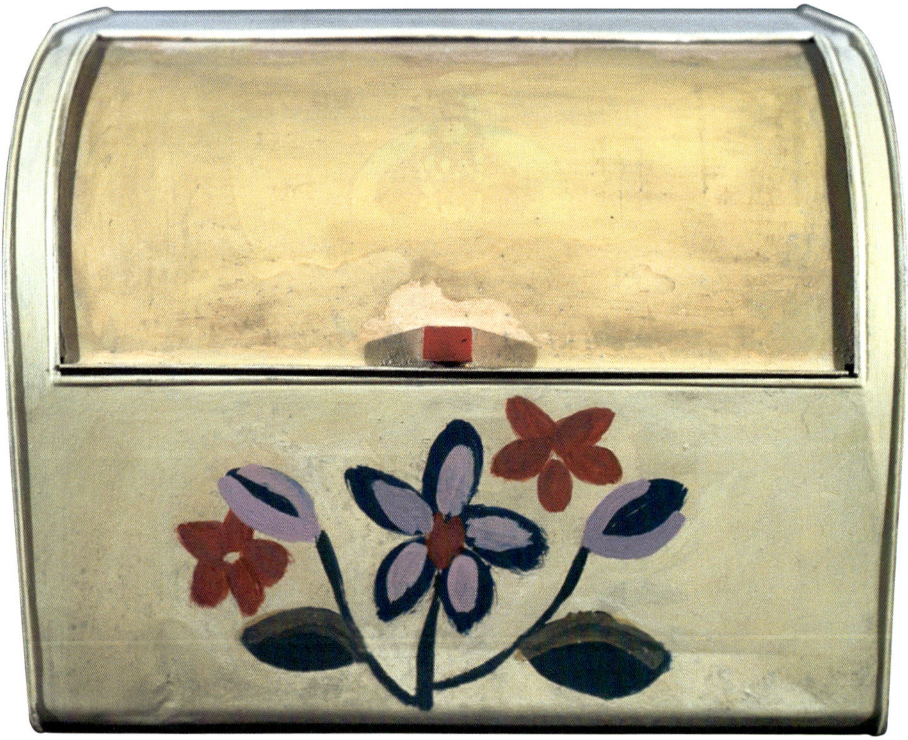

Single-opening breadbox after corrosion removal and cleaning. (Laurie Hamilton)

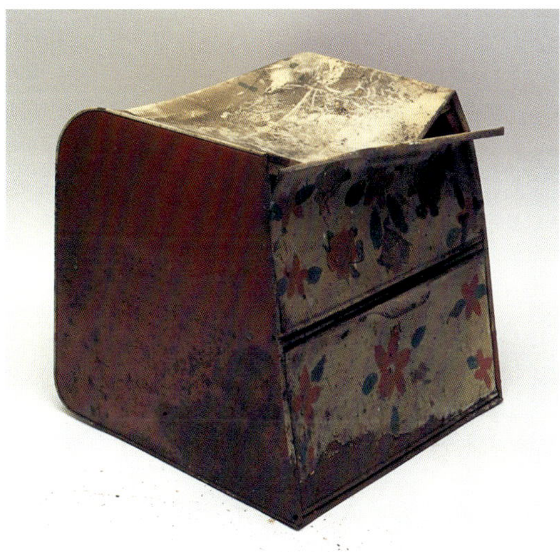

A two-drawer breadbox in poor condition, crushed, dirty, and corroded. (Jennifer McLaughlin)

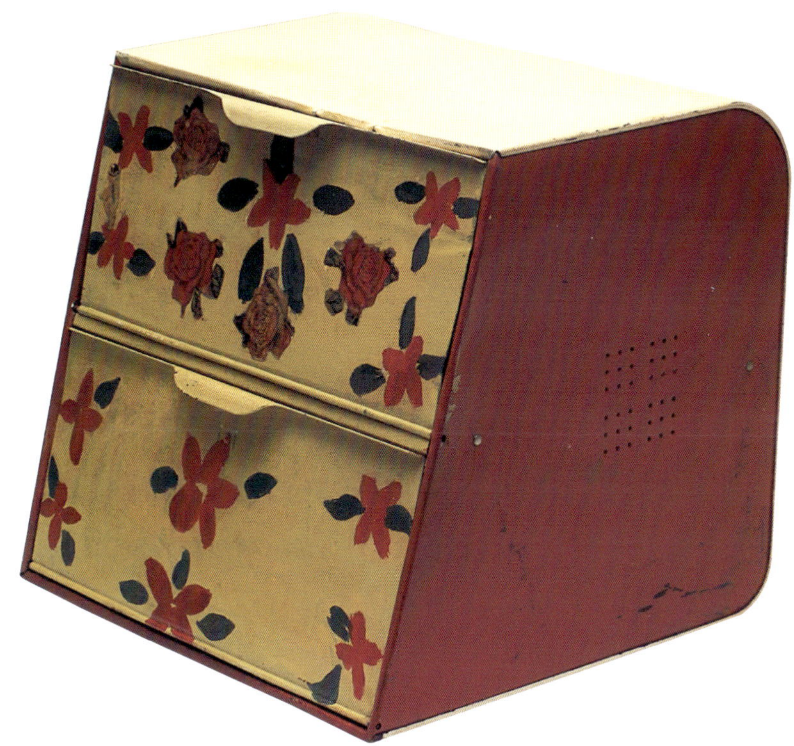

The crushed breadbox had to be reshaped using heat and pressure. (Jennifer McLaughlin)

the bare metal surfaces of the objects with interior cavities: the breadboxes, storage chest, and tea canister. The painted surfaces of the metal objects had offered some protection against rust, but all were affected. On some objects, like the black serving tray and the breadboxes, only speckled clusters of rust had begun to erupt through interstices in the paint layer. Others, like the tea canister and dustpan, were less fortunate: significant amounts of rust covered their entire painted surfaces.

Corrosion on iron and iron alloys is stimulated by moisture and high ambient relative humidity. It can be exacerbated by the presence of environmental salts, which become hygroscopic and attract even more moisture to the surface. These salts originate from human hands, and, not surprisingly, the lid of the tea canister and the handle of the dustpan exhibited the most severe exterior corrosion problems. (When art galleries put up notices asking visitors not to touch the artworks, they are hoping to avoid these environmental salts; they are less fearful of an artwork being broken.)

Corrosion on top of the painted layers had caused some flaking and loss of paint at the fractures in the paint film. Often, it was difficult to tell how much original paint remained in place until the treatment for corrosion removal was underway. Paint losses had also resulted from mechanical damage, such as scratches and abrasion. As well, most of these objects were soiled to varying degrees with a brown layer of oily consistency, composed of cooking oils, wood burning by-products, and nicotine, that had built up over the years. The combination of heavy use and long exposure to uncontrolled environmental conditions had created ideal conditions for rapid corrosion.

Apart from the deterioration associated with corrosion and surface dirt, the top of one of the breadboxes had been severely crushed, presumably from the weight of a heavy object. In order to undo the deformations, we first annealed the metal with heat applied by means of a hot air gun. Holding a custom-made piece of curved aluminum sheeting in place manually against the interior surface, we applied localized pressure to relax the deformations gently. Aluminum was the material of choice for this interior mould, not only for its hardness and rigidity, but for its ability to conduct heat, which allowed the metal to remain malleable while pressure was applied. We used the same process to treat less severe dents and deformations in the other boxes and on the tea canister.

Severe corrosion on the interior bottom surface of one of the food storage boxes suggested that it had served as a cold storage container packed with snow and ice for refrigeration. Maud had decorated this box with decals of snowmen and Santa Claus; the wintry themes reflect the customary use of the box and provide us with a glimpse of her sense of humour. From the perspective of conservation, thin, compact layers of corrosion are considered inactive and, therefore, stable. In some cases, such layers are beneficial as they provide protection for the underlying metal surface. However, the corrosion on the interior of this container was unstable and so advanced that, in some areas, the metal sheet had dissolved completely, leaving holes and perforations.

We used a combination of mechanical and chemical methods of corrosion removal to treat the box. We eliminated the thick and irregular crust of rust using extra fine steel wool (0000 grade) with mineral spirits as a slip agent and degreaser. Next, we placed squares of gelatine containing 10% citric acid on this tin-plated surface as a chemical means of rust removal. The gelatine served as a carrying agent and poultice to hold the acid in close contact with the rust while converting it to a stable, inactive compound. We left this thin, even layer of stable corrosion in place as a protective layer against further possible corrosion.

One of the most attractive objects, both in shape and decoration, is a tin canister that Maud probably used for storing tea. On

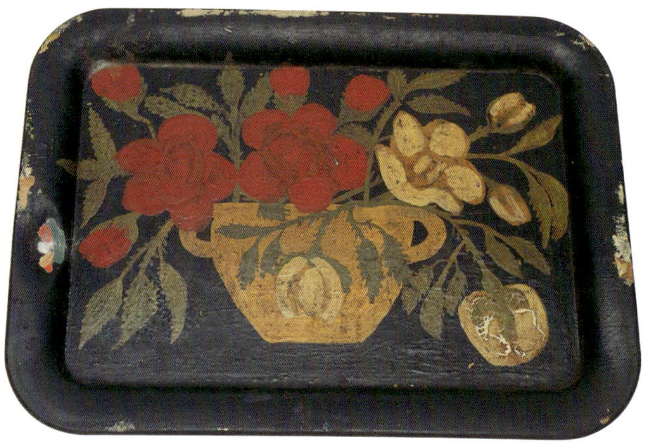

Beautifully painted serving tray with layers of dirt obscuring the original colours Maud had used. (Jennifer McLaughlin)

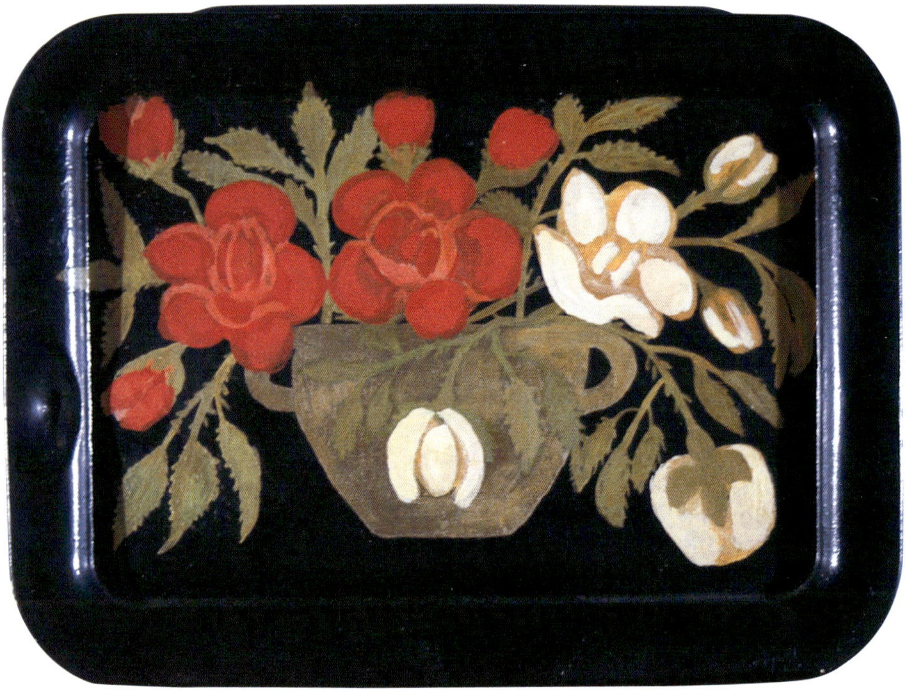

Cleaning reveals the artist's original colours on the tray painted with potted flowers. (Laurie Hamilton)

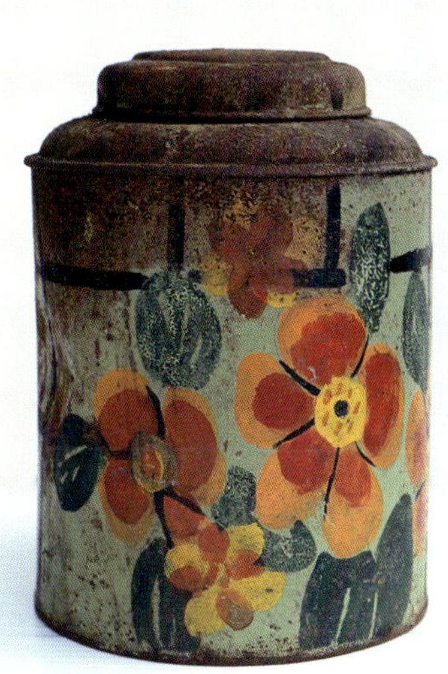

The most severe areas of corrosion on this tea canister occurred primarily where human hands had gripped the container. (Jennifer McLaughlin)

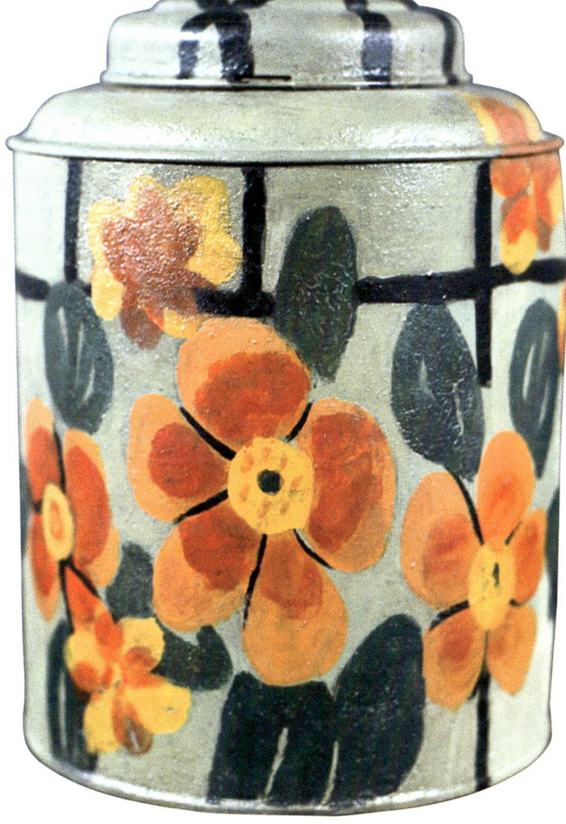

Once the corrosion was removed, the tea canister regained its status as one of the most decoratively painted of the utilitarian objects. (Laurie Hamilton)

a background colour of chrome oxide green, Maud painted a black checkerboard pattern with small floral designs.

Both the interior and exterior surfaces of the tin were severely compromised. Dents and holes, where corrosion had consumed the tin-plated iron sheet, marred the back of the canister. The largest hole was circular and approximately 2.5 cm (1 inch) in diameter.

Preserving as much original material as possible is the paramount principle in the practice of conservation. When treating the corrosion on the painted exteriors of the objects, the preservation of the paint layer below was always a priority for us. Removing rust from the tea canister required great delicacy and finesse because the corrosion had broken through the paint layer and continued to form over and around it. We decided that the traditional mechanical method of fine steel wool and mineral spirits would be too abrasive. Instead, we used a mesh pad (3M Scotchbrite) with mineral spirits. These pads are made from woven nylon mesh and allow for gentle removal of the corrosion without scratching or damaging the paint surface. As the corrosion removal progressed and the rust layer grew thinner, we were pleased to discover that most of the original paint was still present and intact underneath. We then patched the holes in the metal on the back of the canister using Araldite putty, a thermosetting epoxy resin compound that does not react with the metal.

After the corrosion removal and stabilisation phase of the treatment was completed, we were faced with the problem of cleaning away the layers of surface dirt and accretions from the metal objects. Given the oily nature of this layer, for most of the objects we used an aqueous alkaline solution with a pH of 8.5. Naturally, we did extensive testing first to determine the correct solution, one that allowed the safe removal of the dirt layer without affecting the paint layer. The aqueous alkaline solution was an especially good choice because it was completely volatile and left no residue behind. Once we had removed the oily outermost layer of surface dirt, we did further cleaning of each object using a complexing solution of water to which a 5% chelating agent, DPTA-diethylene petra-acetic acid sodium salt in this instance, was added. The chelating agent is a chemical scavenger for metal ions, binding up the remaining metal ions of rust which could then be rinsed away from the surface using deionised water.

Finally, because of losses in the paint surface of all the metal objects, we retouched each object as necessary to reintegrate the design and restore visual harmony, using custom blends of dry pigments mixed with a non-yellowing synthetic resin binder, Berger's Inpainting Medium, a polyvinyl acetate resin in solvent.

Two-Dimensional Objects

Maud's colourful basket of daisies set against a vibrant red background represents one of her most innovative choices of substrate upon which to paint: a rectangular piece of linoleum (rubber/tar composite) whose tattered, irregular edges under the paint layers tell us of its worn state even when she commenced her work.

As usual, Maud's paint medium was a combination of industrial oils and alkyds. The paint was thickly applied but appeared to be smooth and glossy beneath layers of dirt and accretions. It was coated with what appeared to be an oil-based layer that had discoloured with age to a rich yellow hue. Apart from an oily brown layer of surface soil, the major problem confronting us was flaking paint.

With age, the paint surface had developed a fine pattern of hairline cracks almost like those that can develop on an eggshell. On traditional oil paintings on canvas, this type of craquelure in the paint film is often perfectly stable. In the case of the linoleum support, however, with each crack, a small loss of paint had occurred. As well, the linoleum had developed some gentle planar distortions, but even

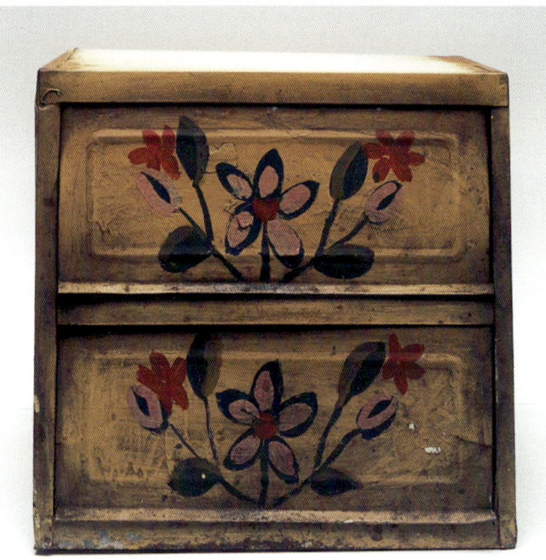

This second double-drawer breadbox sat beneath the single drawer unit, accounting for the matching floral motifs. (Jennifer McLaughlin)

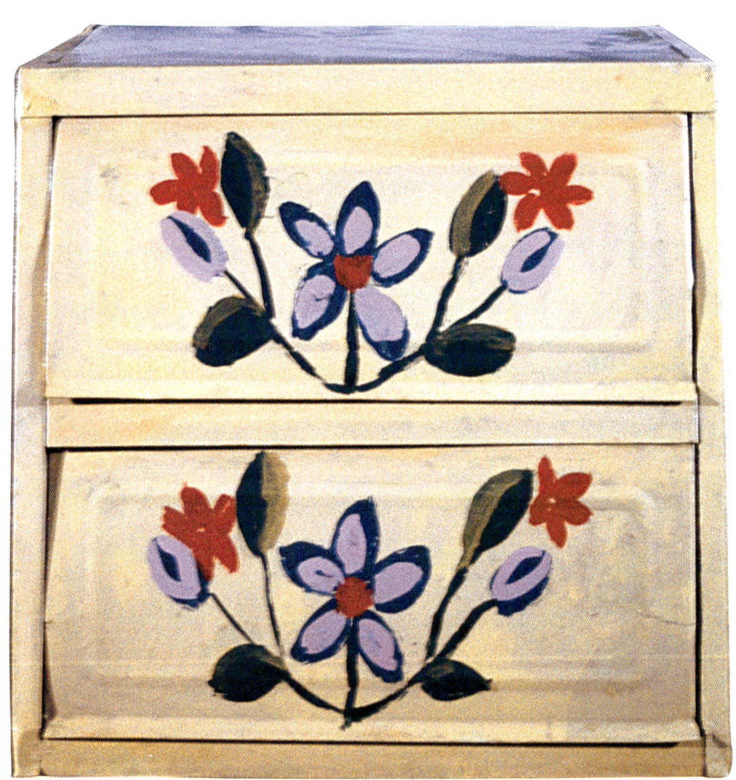

Two-drawer breadbox, after treatment. (Laurie Hamilton)

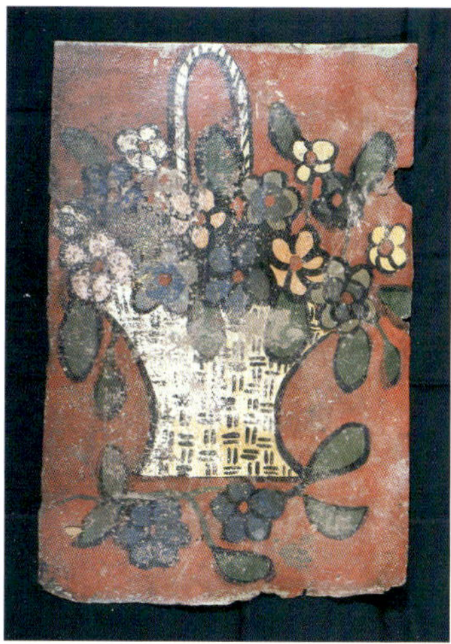

Dirt and multiple paint losses marred this decorative painted basket of flowers executed on a scrap of linoleum. (Laurie Hamilton)

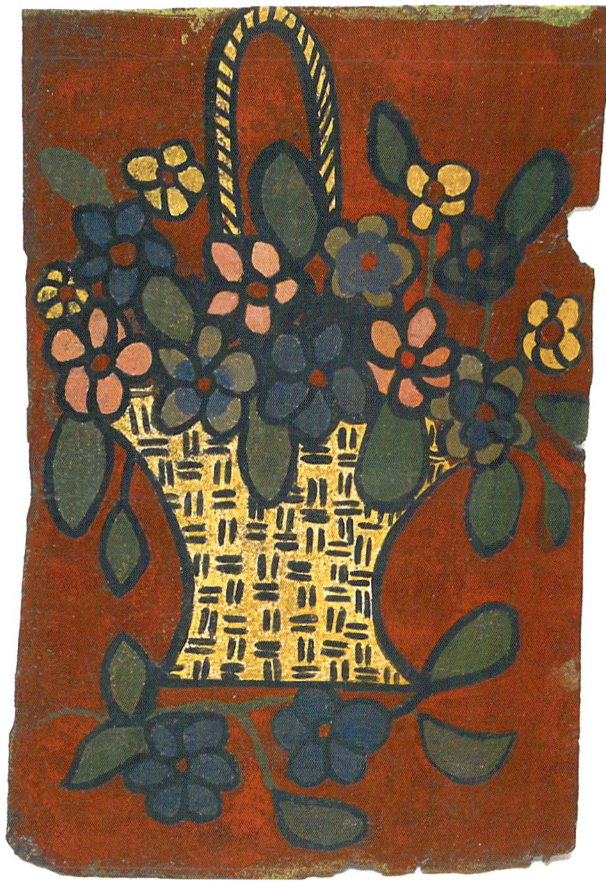

The painting on linoleum after treatment. (Jennifer McLaughlin)

this small movement in the substrate exacerbated the flaking problem. The paint losses were small in size but great in number, most occurring in the upper left quadrant as viewed from the front.

Flaking paint layers of this magnitude required immediate consolidation. Fortunately, the paint that remained on the surface seemed stable enough to allow cleaning as a first step. Initially, we used mechanical methods, removing the loose and powdery dirt and dust with a soft-bristle brush. Next, we tried the pH neutral vulcanized latex sponges, known as Wishab Sponges, which proved effective in removing the less powdery layers of oily dirt that were loosely adhered to the surface.

Treatment of this piece was complicated by the presence of an irregularly applied coating that appeared to be oil-based. This deep yellow layer remained well adhered to the surface of the paint. Over this was a moderate to heavy layer of greasy dark brown dirt, likely the result of soot and wood burning by-products from the nearby stove. We tested the painting for aqueous surface cleaning and chose to use saliva, applied with cotton swabs to one small section at a time, each then cleared with deionised water. The enzymes in the saliva were particularly effective in breaking down the oily dirt layers. We next tested for removal of the yellowed surface coating. Given the sensitive nature of the red paint Maud had used for the background, we opted for partial, rather than complete, removal of this layer. Using a 1% aqueous alkaline solution with added surfactant of Triton x-100, we reduced this layer to an even thickness over the entire surface. This reduction of the discoloured layer allowed a rebalancing of tonal values: the red background lost its orange appearance, and the whites of the flower petals emerged once again from their yellow veil.

Approaching the end of the treatment, we consolidated the surface with a brush coating of 12% B-72, a synthetic resin composed of methyl ethyl methacrylate dissolved in xylene, which also served as an isolating layer to separate subsequent fills from the original linoleum surface. The most visually distracting losses were filled with putty consisting of a mixture of calcium carbonate and Moviol (polyvinyl alcohol), smoothed to match the surrounding paint surface, and inpainted. The less obtrusive ones were left unfilled to maintain the patina of age and wear that had taken place even during Maud's lifetime. The need for delicate filling and precise colour-matching was extremely time-consuming. As a final protective barrier, we sprayed on a very thin layer of Regalrez 1094, a synthetic hydrocarbon resin to which Tinuvin 292 has been added as a hindered amine light stabilizer. This would buffer the damaging effects of ultraviolet light.

Maud also painted on scraps of stiff cardboard using the same industrial oils and alkyds that she had used elsewhere. One particularly attractive work is a vertical composition featuring a pot of long-stemmed tulips painted in rich, glossy oil paint with no background colour other than that of the natural board.

The paint was lifting slightly around several holes, some as large as 3 cm (1¼ inches) in diameter, caused by nail heads pulling through the cardboard. The surface of the image was soiled with an even layer of dark greyish dirt.

The dry cleaning of uncoated paper substrates requires gentle conservation materials. We employed molecular trap rubbers known as Groomstick to remove the loose dirt safely from the bare cardboard. The oil-painted design was carefully cleaned using cotton swabs dipped in an aqueous solution with surfactant as used previously. We consolidated the holes in the cardboard with wheat starch paste and patched them from the reverse using linen archival repair tape. We filled the slight depression left with acrylic cellulose and inpainted these areas with watercolours to match the colour and the matte surface of the cardboard. Synthetic resin and dry pigments were used to in-paint the losses in the tulips.

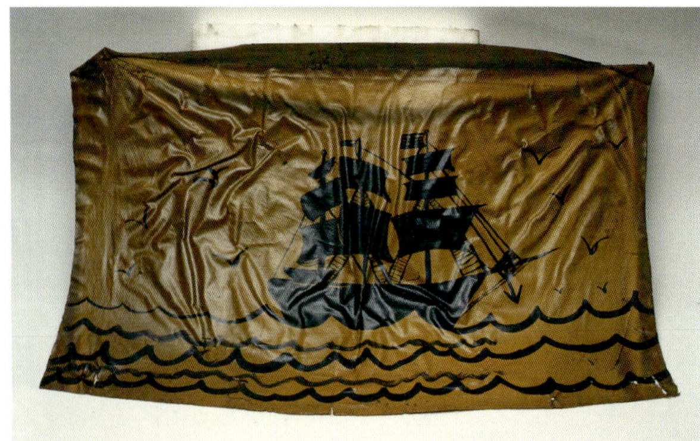

Pinned at its corners on the sloping ceiling in the attic, the painting of a black ship was extremely disfigured with planar distortions. (Jennifer McLaughlin)

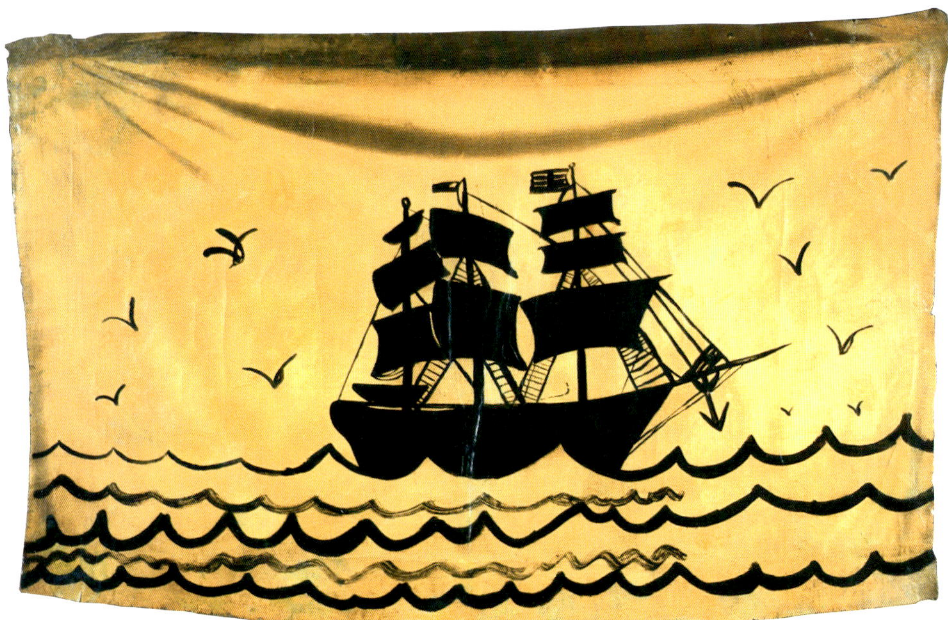

Dramatic in its effect, the black ship against a yellow background, shown here after treatment, was a subject repeated by Maud on other surfaces. (Laurie Hamilton)

The closest thing to traditional artists' canvas that Maud ever used as a painting support was oilcloth. This open-weave fabric was extremely thin, little more than gauze. The commercially applied oil-based coating supplied the fabric with its only strength. Maud painted two compositions on rectangular pieces of such oilcloth. The most dramatic is a black, silhouetted image of a sailing ship at sea set against a yellow background. Perhaps she intended this colour palette to convey the haunting atmosphere of dusk at sea.

The fabric support was in poor condition, with a number of planar deformations in the form of a regular series of drooping undulations. The painting had been pinned to the wall in the upstairs attic with a tack in each corner. As the fabric sagged with time, the original oil coating, as well as Maud's application of paint, polymerized and hardened, forming rigid deformations. The paint layers had cracked, especially in the folds of the cloth. A number of small tears and surface abrasions further marred the surface. The reverse of the cloth was exceptionally dirty, covered in a thick, even layer of dry accretions.

After cleaning the surface with dry brushes and Wishab Sponges, our primary task was to relax the distortions in the fabric. Given the state of embrittlement, the only way to introduce flexibility was through moisture. We reinforced the edges of the oilcloth with strips of polyester fabric (Dacron) attached to the underside edges using BEVA 371, a reversible thermoplastic adhesive. We then loosely stretched the painting on a temporary strainer, using thumbtacks to hold the Dacron in place on the turnover edges. The strainer with the attached canvas was then placed into a humidity chamber. As the fabric gradually took up moisture, we gradually increased the tension of the canvas on the strainer gradually to ease out the draws and distortions. When the draws were comfortably removed from the canvas, we released the painting from the wooden strainer, removed two of the four Dacron strips, and removed the adhesive with mineral spirits. The oilcloth painting was then allowed to equilibrate to the normal environmental humidity of the gallery. We left the remaining two strips of Dacron, on the top and bottom of the cloth, in place to serve as reinforcement for future handling and mounting and as the basis for the repair of the small tears along the top and bottom edges.

We cleaned the surface of the painting with an aqueous alkaline solution, which removed a great deal of oily greyish dirt, and applied an overall layer of consolidating resin (10% B-72) to stabilize the cracking in the paint layer. The paint losses were then filled and inpainted, as was done for the linoleum artifact.

Using the same type of oilcloth support, Maud painted a bouquet of red flowers above a checkerboard pattern running across the lower portion of the fabric.

This piece did not suffer from the same hardened draws as the painting of the black ship; it was, however, badly torn, with a 7.5 cm (3 inch) vertical tear and a 1 centimetre (½ inch) loss of canvas in an aperture at the upper centre of the composition. After giving the piece a general cleaning and relaxing the gentle undulations in the oilcloth support, we mended the tear by bridging the fibres with a nylon welding powder designed for textile restoration. Next, we patched the tear from the reverse using polyester fabric adhered with Lascaux 360, a reversible contact adhesive emulsion. We used the same filling and inpainting techniques as before.

Painted Stairs

Maud even painted the stairs to the house's small attic. All but the bottom two risers were painted with decorative floral designs of forget-me-not-style flowers in shades of blue, cream, and light green, arranged in dark, rectangular containers reminiscent of window boxes. A regular pattern of craquelure in the floral designs probably developed during the drying process, within months of Maud's painting them. The cracks are not visually distracting and remain indicative of both the artist's technique and the environmental conditions within the house.

Apart from a loose handrail, the hardwood staircase was sound and stable. The painted design layers were in good condition and seemed well adhered to the wooden substrate. Various losses and abrasions in the paint surface, particularly along the treads, no doubt represent normal usage where toes and heels of shoes came in contact. A dark, oily, yellowish layer of dirt and accretions, forming a patchy coating overall, disfigured the staircase and hid the sparkling array of colours Maud had applied.

An aqueous solution of Orvus, a neutral synthetic anionic detergent (sodium lauryl sulfate) applied with large cotton swabs and cleared away with distilled water, removed a considerable amount of greyish-brown dirt. A second cleaning, using an aqueous solution with a slightly higher pH to break down the oily layer, achieved dramatic results, lifting away the dingy dirt layer and revealing the bright yellow and blue tones beneath. We consolidated unstable paint around the areas of loss with B-72 acrylic resin introduced under the lifting paint with a fine brush and capillary action. After filling areas of loss with acrylic cellulose and using a damp chamois wrapped around a felt block to smooth the surfaces, we inpainted these fills using polyvinyl acetate with dry pigments to complete the treatment.

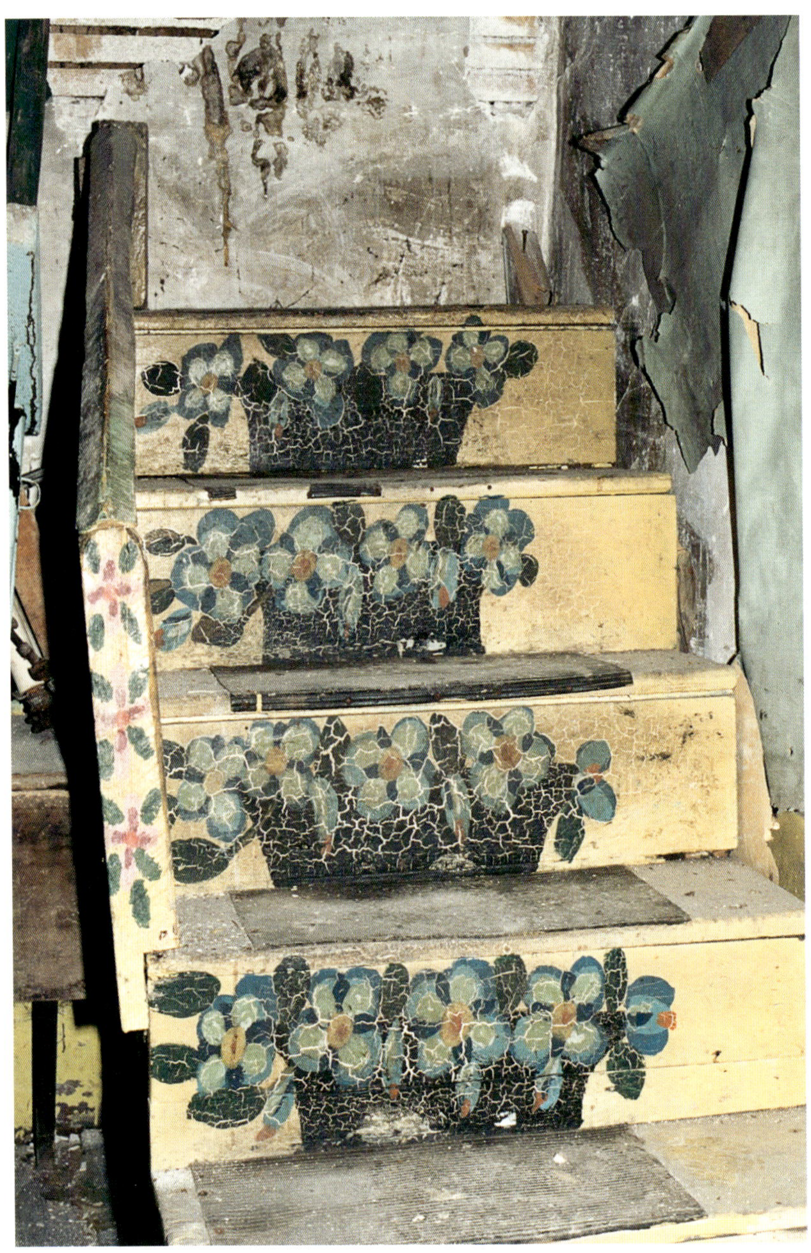

With her debilitating arthritis, executing the repeated images of blue forget-me-not flowers on the stair risers must have been a difficult physical challenge for Maud. (Craig Dix)

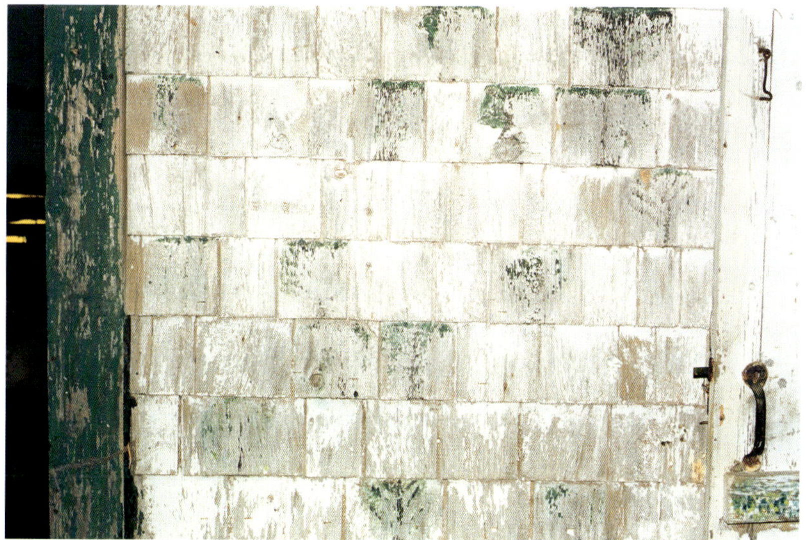

The evergreen trees that Everett painted on the front facade after Maud's death suffered extensive loss as a result of weathering. (Craig Dix)

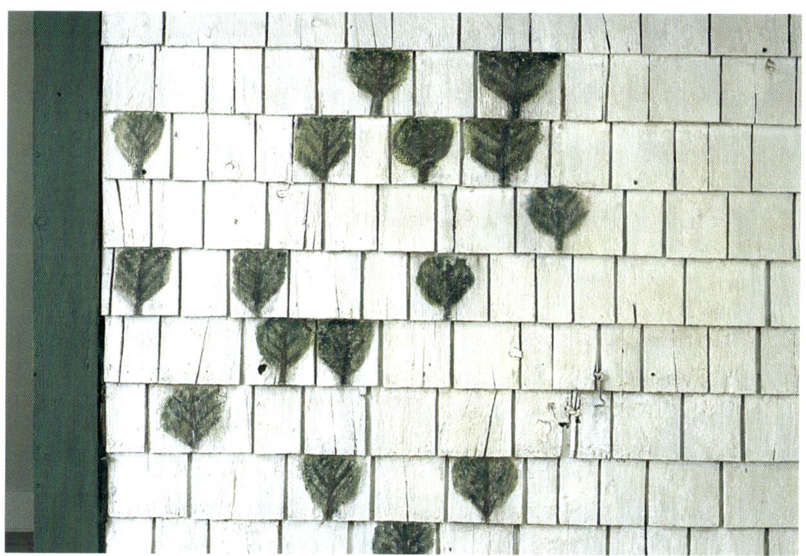

The missing areas of the evergreen tree images were reconstructed using archival photographs as reference. (Gary Castle)

Painted Exterior Walls

The exterior of the little house was shingled and painted white, with the later addition of twenty-five small evergreen trees, painted by Everett after Maud's death, scattered randomly on the front facade. The simple colour scheme for the decoration used only two tones of green for the foliage and a brown for the trunks.

Over the years, wind and rain had eroded the paint layer and left what remained of the white background heavily soiled with mud and salt stains. Although faint, outlines of the decorative trees remained, enough to allow for a full restoration of the missing areas to re-integrate the design.

We began by mechanically cleaning the exterior walls, using a dry brush and vacuum to lift away all the dirt, accretions, and loose paint from the crevices of the shingles, taking care not to affect the areas of painted decoration. Again using Orvus detergent, we were able to remove a great deal of dirt as well as the salt stains. We could then assess the exterior appearance of the house and compare it to photographs taken in the late 1970s, when Everett lived there on his own. To upgrade the bare appearance of the walls and to achieve harmonious balance in the white paint required only a light sponging of dilute acrylic emulsion white paint, toned down to give an aged appearance with the addition of raw umber and sienna. The excess was immediately wiped off the areas of pre-existing paint; this allowed us to cover raw exposed wood with a translucent white layer while leaving areas of original paint intact. With the aid of archival photographs, we inpainted the decorative evergreen trees to reproduce the exact patterning and colours that Everett had completed in the 1970s. The medium used was polyvinyl acetate resin in solvent with custom-blended dry pigments. Microballoons were added to create a matte appearance.

The Sunnyside Mall Workplace

Working in a mall conjures up images of pressing crowds and an unfocussed work environment, but nothing could be further from reality. During the expansion of the Sunnyside Mall in Bedford, Nova Scotia, the management provided a partially completed section where the house could be treated behind a glass barrier in full view of the public. On their work breaks, the conservators could talk with members of the public or answer their questions about conservation techniques. Many of the mall visitors had known Maud or had enjoyed some personal connection to her tiny house, and we felt privileged to share their many fond memories and stories about her. During time-sensitive procedures when we were unable to take a break, staff at the small AGNS Gallery Shop gift kiosk nearby were able to greet the public and answer questions about our work. This friendly and welcoming atmosphere formed a pleasant contrast to our usual isolation in the conservation lab at a museum.

Conservation and Restoration of the Wallpaper

The wallpapers used to decorate Maud's house no doubt reflect Everett's ability to scrounge roll-ends rather than their conscious choice. The three separate wallpaper treatments in the house each demanded individual consideration: two required replication methods and the third involved detailed conservation and restoration techniques.

The first to be tackled was a commercially manufactured paper, found on the south and west walls, with a small abstract pattern in green and brown tones. Because the wall plaster was in such poor condition, only small remnants of the paper were salvageable. We decided to see whether modern catalogues could closely approximate the original pattern. This task, though not difficult, was time-consuming and gave rise to a new appreciation for the sheer quantity of pattern books and the range of wallpaper designs produced today. After much searching and deliberation, we found a pattern that had the desired overall effect. Once applied to the two walls using standard wallpapering techniques, a scumble of acrylic pigments (raw umber, yellow ochre, and mars black) was thinly applied to simulate the years of accumulated soot and dirt deposits.

The second area of concern was a small section behind Maud's TV table, where another commercial wallpaper featuring green ivy on a complex grid of grey, red, and tan stripes was situated. Although a plethora of ivy-based wallpaper prints remains popular, none came close to the appearance of this particular pattern. Modern

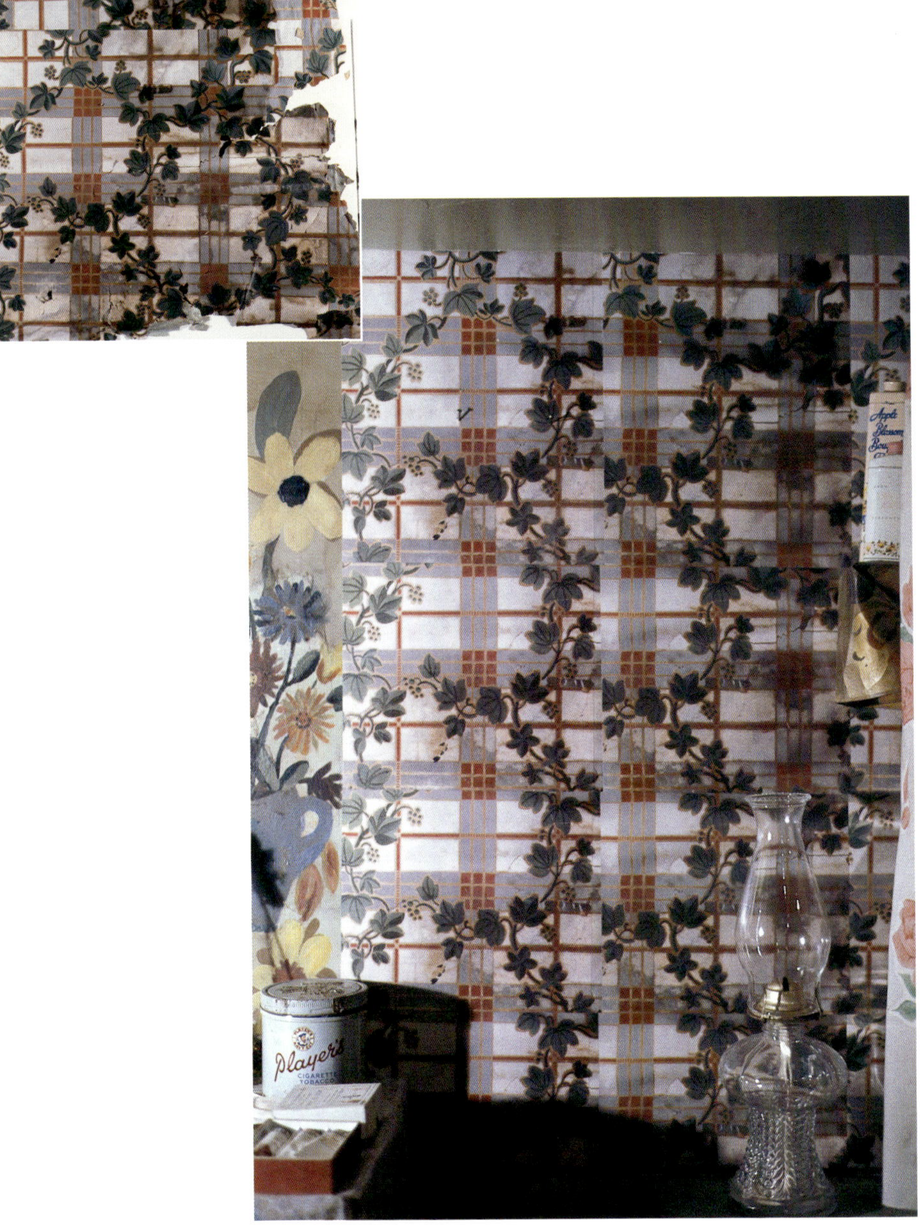

The large remnant of ivy-patterned wallpaper (left) was photo-reproduced, and copies were spliced together to simulate the original appearance of the wall section immediately behind Maud's TV table (right). (Laurie Hamilton)

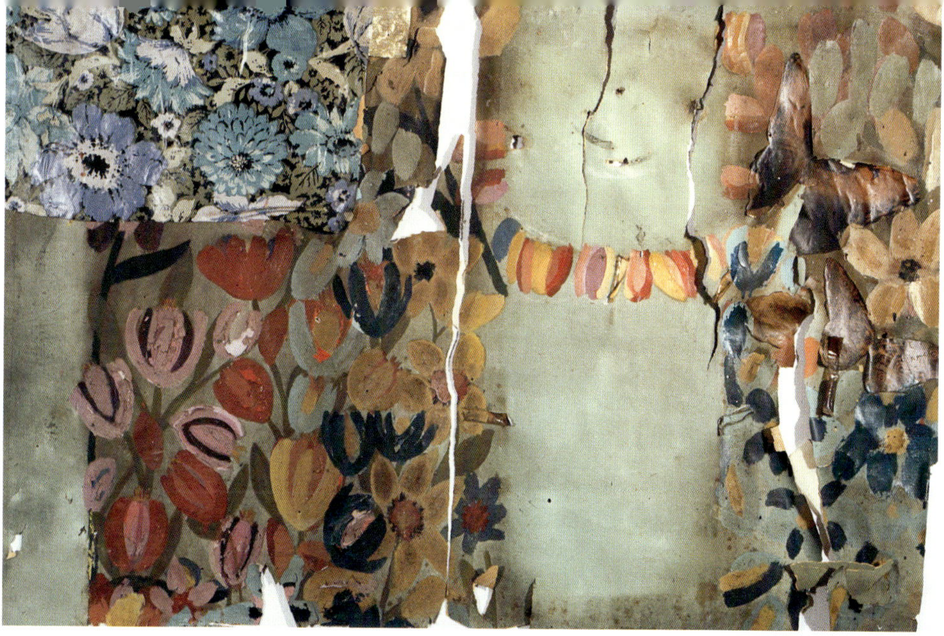

A section of the hand-painted wallpaper on the east wall in its before-treatment condition. (Jennifer McLaughlin)

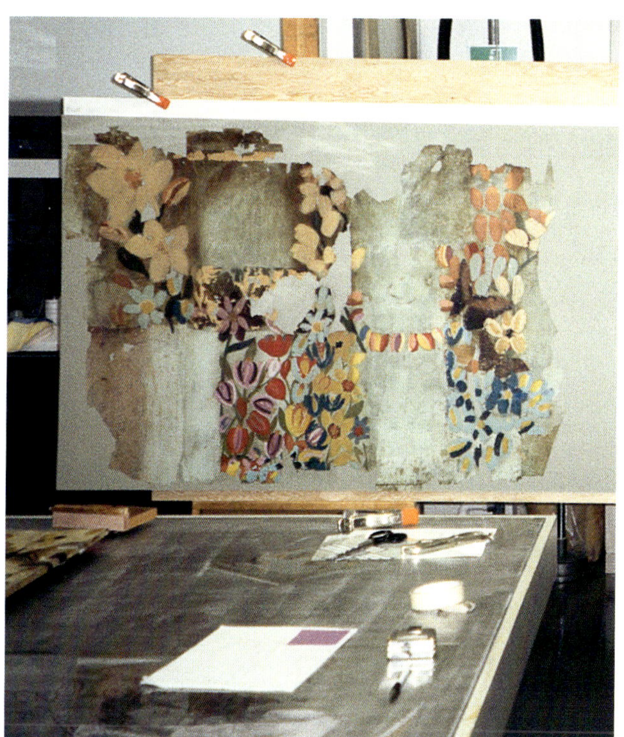

The same section of wallpaper in the AGNS conservation lab, after washing, cleaning, and mounting on the composite support system. (Laurie Hamilton)

technology provided us with the eventual solution. Using the large remaining fragment, six full-scale colour photocopies were made and spliced together in a manner that simulated the size and repeat pattern of the original. The addition of the hand-painted mirror which Maud had positioned over this wallpaper and the distance of the photocopies from the viewing point allow them to work well and proved them the ideal solution to this particular problem.

The third challenge was fundamental to the success of the overall conservation and restoration of the house interior because it involved the two stunning walls of hand-painted wallpaper, completed by the artist over a grey-green background paper. Only half the original paper had survived the ravages of time, and that in an extreme state of deterioration. The significant topmost layer was attached to many underlying layers of commercial wallpaper of no artistic consequence. This laminate of paper and adhesive was brittle, discoloured, torn, acidified, and severely out of plane. The paint media, a combination of industrial alkyd and oil paints, remained well adhered to the substrate for the most part, and the tough nature of these paints permitted the cautious use of dry and wet paper conservation procedures. The surface generally was heavily soiled with a dark grey deposit indicative of an accumulation of soot and nicotine particulate.

Cleaning the wallpaper involved the use of several specialized commercial materials designed specifically for dry removal of loosely adhered surface dirt. Groomstick, a molecular trap rubber which lifts dirt away rather than rubbing it off, Wishab Sponges, and white vinyl erasers were all used. The colours brightened considerably after gentle cleaning with a combination of these products.

The fragments were then float-washed in a distilled water bath using a screen support system to ensure safe handling during this delicate procedure. The water softened the glue which bound the many layers of wallpaper together and allowed the separation of the

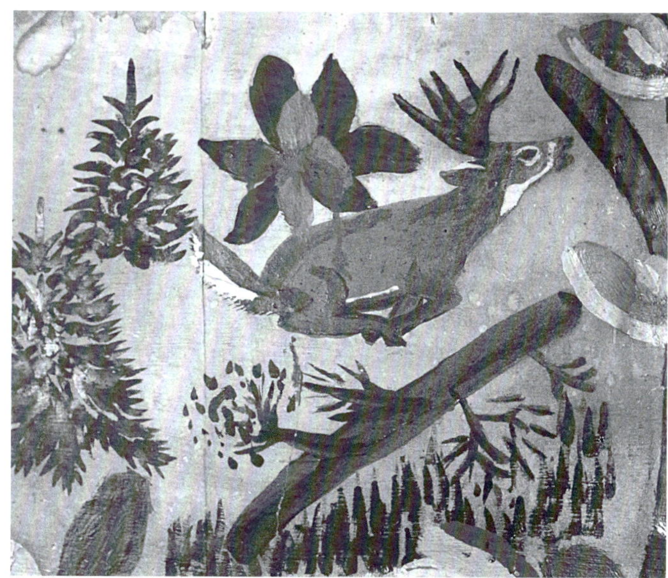

Original section of wallpaper design which Everett sold after Maud's death. Collection of George Fraser. (Laurie Hamilton)

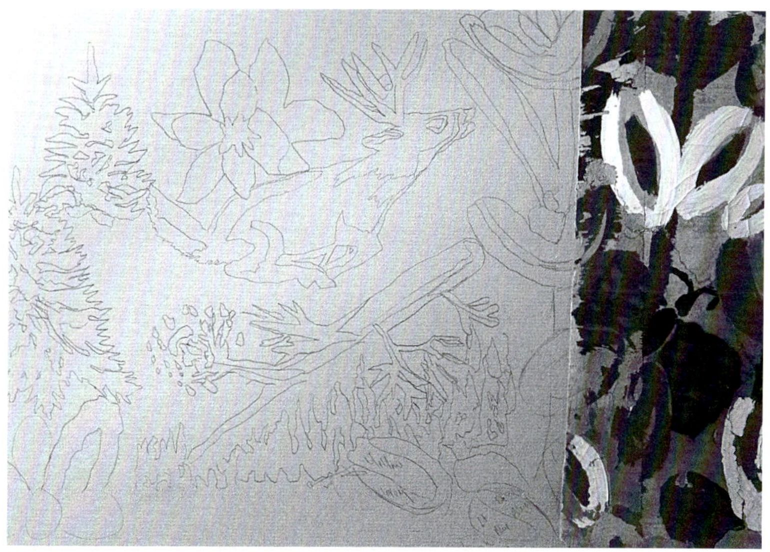

The pencil drawing of the missing section of wallpaper as it was reconstructed using projected archival slides. (Laurie Hamilton)

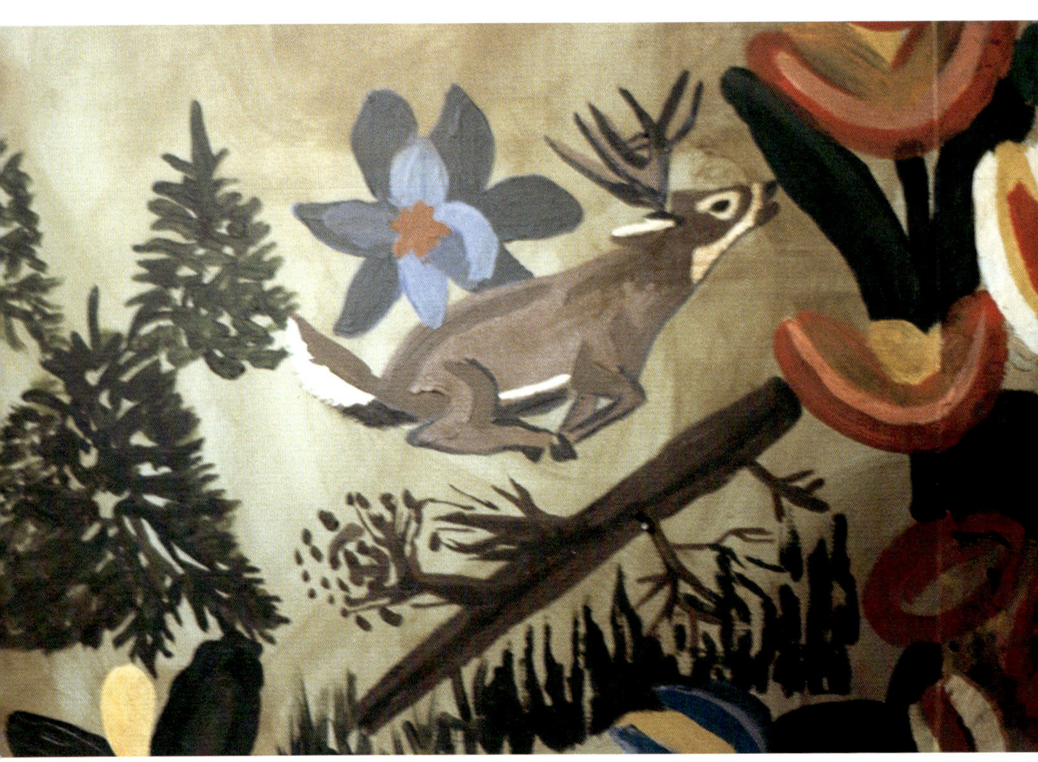

Acrylic paints were used to inpaint the missing images. A thin wash of toned medium simulated the aged appearance of the originals. (Laurie Hamilton)

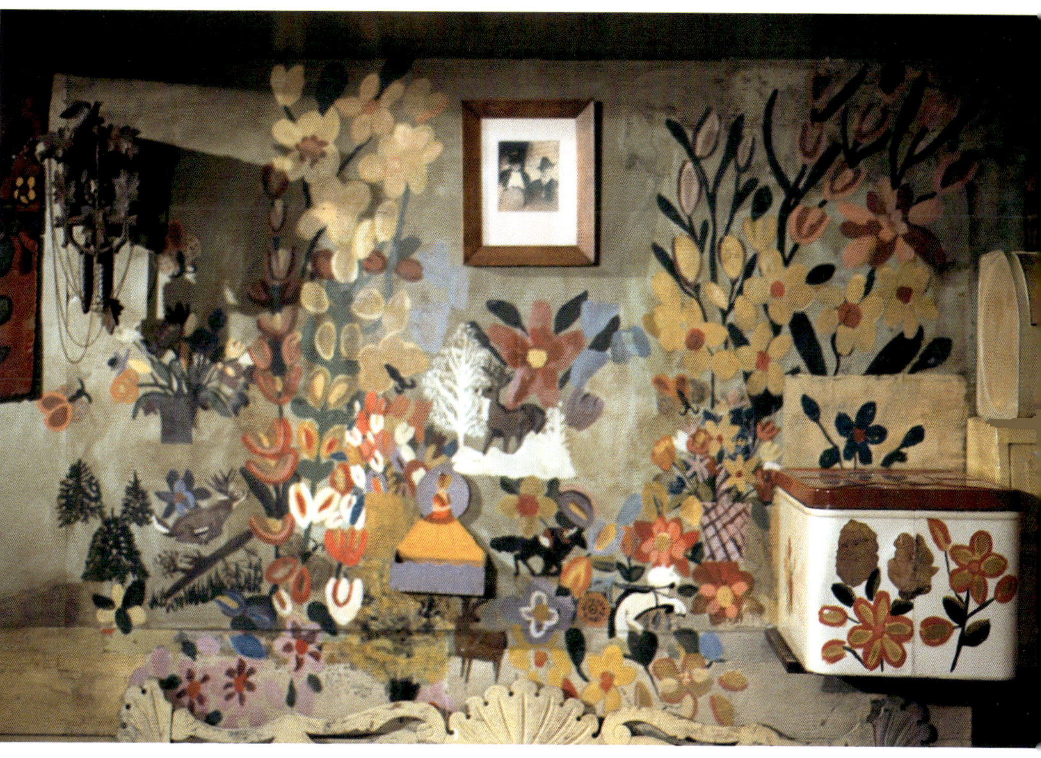

Overall view of the north wall after restoration of the wallpaper. (Laurie Hamilton)

hand-painted upper sheet from the underlying layers. Fortuitously, it also encouraged some dissolution of water-soluble acids and dirt within the paper matrix. The paper was placed between acid-free blotters, glass sheets, and weights to allow for controlled drying in a flat plane.

We considered numerous possible mounting systems for the replacement of the wallpaper in the house and finally chose a composite support system designed with 6 millimetre (¼ inch) sheets of white Foamcore, a pH neutral board with a buffered paper enclosing an extruded polystyrene core, as the base. Foamcore comes in large four-by-eight sheets, making it an ideal material to cover the surface area of the walls above the wainscotting. An acid-free museum mat board of an appropriate colour to blend with the green-grey of the original was adhered to this using dilute polyvinyl acetate emulsion glue. A conservation adhesive known as BEVA Gel, an aqueous dispersion of ethylene vinyl acetate and acrylic resins, was used to secure the paper fragments to the support system.

Once the wallpaper was attached to the supports, the existing images were traced onto mylar overlays so that we could piece together the missing ones from the archive of colour slides available. Having completed as full a representation for both walls as possible, we were ready to confront the next stage of transferring the images to be replicated to the composite board. Appropriate slides were projected onto the support system, adjusting the position and angle of the projector to compensate for image distortion produced by the angle at which the photographs were originally taken, until registration with the existing images was achieved. The missing areas were outlined using pencil with colour-coding notes added for later reference.

Enlarged photographs made from the crucial slides provided great assistance in the colour replication stage of the treatment. The lost images were recreated using water-based acrylic paints in combination with acrylic thickeners to simulate the areas of higher impasto. Care was taken to duplicate the darkened appearance of the original wallpaper using the same scumble of brown and black pigments. Our goal was to merge the new and original sections of wallpaper effectively from a distance of 2 to 3 metres (about 6 to 10 feet), roughly the distance at which viewers would look into the house, and in this we were successful. On closer scrutiny, the replicated images can be easily distinguished from the authentic material. Proper registration of the wallpaper panels was fairly straightforward, since we could use shadow lines and other visual clues, such as the body of the deer on the lower wainscotting, which obviously had to align with the head portion on the wallpaper above.

Installation of the panels was more of a challenge. On the north and east walls, in place of plaster, 6 millimetre (¼ inch) plywood was screwed to the studs to form a secure base for attachment of the Foamcore panels. The uneven plaster application, which simulated the look of the old ceiling, necessitated a labour-intensive process of channelling a groove at the wall-ceiling interface into which the panels could slide and ultimately rest on the boards of the wainscotting below. Preparators screwed brass mending plates through the panels into the plywood in discreet areas where a decorative object would eventually be hung, ensuring security of the system but not interfering with the continuity of the overall visual effect.

With the addition of the many decorative materials, including a number of Maud's flower paintings and other two-dimensional materials, the walls resonate with visual impact and are unquestionably significant components in the successful presentation of the Maud Lewis Painted House.

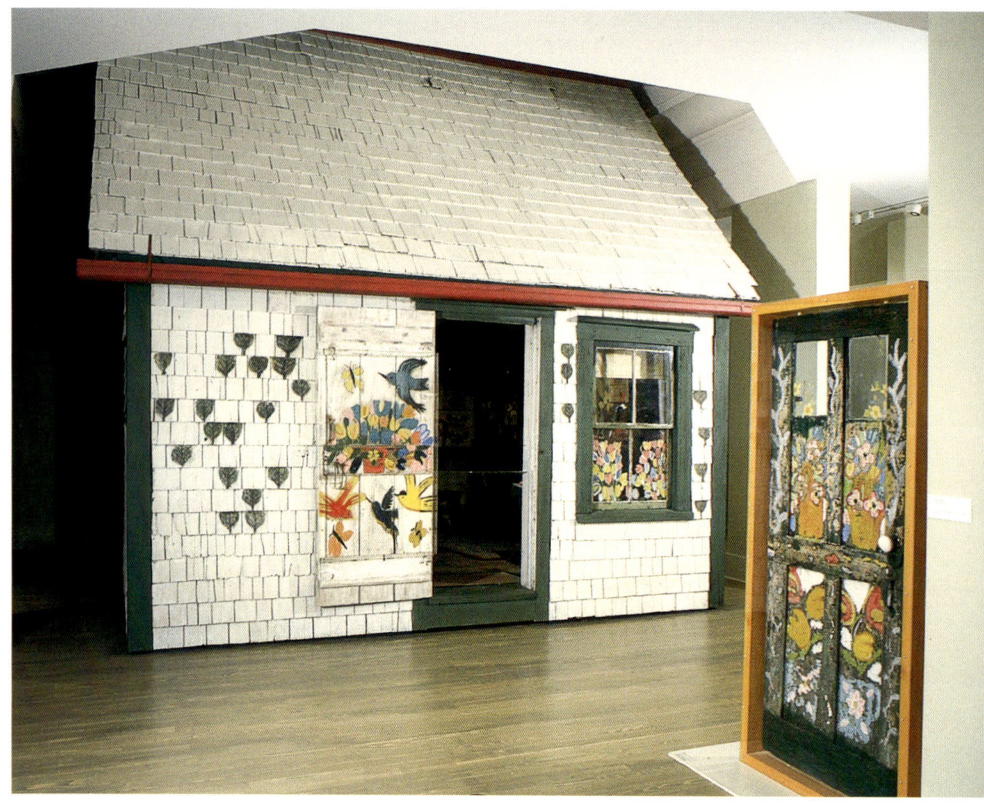

The Maud Lewis Painted House as it now looks in the Scotiabank Maud Lewis Gallery. (G.N. Hilfiker)

A New Home for the House

Decisions about final installation details and the configuration of the surrounding display area brought this conservation project to its conclusion. Staff members from the departments of education, programming, conservation, and gallery services met to discuss possibilities and reach consensus on the appropriateness of the display and on the use of didactic and interactive materials that would create an informative and enjoyable exhibition.

Fortunately, a large quantity of original materials relating to Maud's painting technique and her mail-order business had survived and could be re-introduced into the corner area where the artist produced her small paintings: paint brushes, paint tubes, and all manner of recycled cans for mixing pots were repositioned on the window ledge and metal TV table where she had used them. The many letters from patrons requesting paintings of a certain subject, often with an uncashed cheque enclosed, were replaced on the shelving unit next to her paint table, poignant reminders that, with worsening health, Maud often found it difficult to keep up with the demand for her life-affirming art.

The furniture, mostly original to the house, was in need of cleaning and minor consolidation only. Everett's penchant for painting the wainscotting on the house in multiple tones of yellow and green, without first moving furnishings out of the way, left little question as to the positioning of certain key items like the upholstered daybed and drop-leaf table.

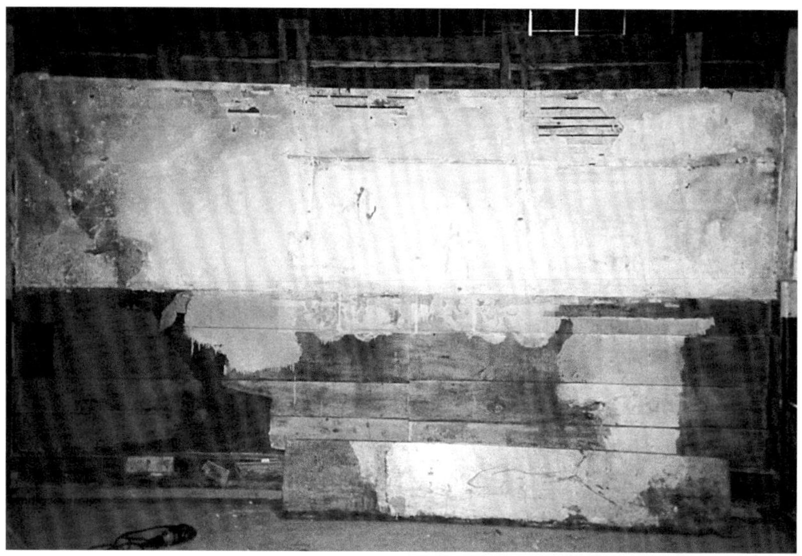

Everett unwittingly aided the restoration process with his penchant for painting around furnishings. Here a perfect silhouette of the staircase and the back of the daybed on the north wall leaves their exact location for the final display in no doubt. (Jennifer McLaughlin)

Not surprisingly, much of the textile material, including hooked mats, curtains, bedspread, and plastic shelf covers, did not survive. Where possible, we replaced these with others closely approximating the look of the originals: old hooked mats were purchased from a local antique dealer, and a vintage bedspread was generously donated to the cause. Fabric stores today still stock period-style plastic shelf coverings with lace and floral patterns; the judicious application of a pigmented wash to simulate age made these modern substitutes blend unnoticeably into the general ambience of the house interior.

The dilemma of what to do at the house entrance concerned us for some time. For the security and safety of fragile objects within so confined a space, we agreed that visitors would view the interior from the entranceway but would not be allowed access into the house. A sliding half-panel of Plexiglas discreetly blocks the door opening, preventing entry without obstructing a good view of the interior. Plexiglas covers over the fragile designs on the storm door and windows also afford protection from wayward hands. The beautifully painted panelled door was problematic: how could people enjoy a view of both sides if it were rehung on the house? Our compromise solution was to place the door in its own custom-built enclosure, close to but separate from the house, where front and back could be studied and enjoyed equally.

In the gallery space surrounding the house, we designed areas where visitors can access an educational and interactive CD ROM about Maud Lewis (available for purchase) at a computer terminal, or watch the National Film Board's delightful documentary video, *A World Without Shadows*, in an adjacent sitting space. A comprehensive display of Maud's paintings, interspersed with text panels chronicling her life and achievements, adorns the gallery walls, as do many of the charming photographs of Maud, Everett, and the Painted House so ably taken by Bob Brooks in 1965.

It is an exciting and sometimes unsettling challenge to put together an exhibition that can meet a variety of expectations. Since the Scotiabank Maud Lewis Gallery opened in June of 1998, it has been a rewarding experience to read about reactions to the house installation in the hundreds of comments recorded by its visitors. Without question, the story of Maud Lewis and the legacy of her painted house inspire a strong reaction in people of all ages. Schoolchildren relate to its scale and simplicity, while adults often feel a connection to Maud's spirit still present in her house. It is fitting that a sampling of these personal reactions should end this text.

> *I am completely touched both by her life portrait as well as her work — her creativity, her need to express herself visually was so much a part of her spiritual response to what others might consider*

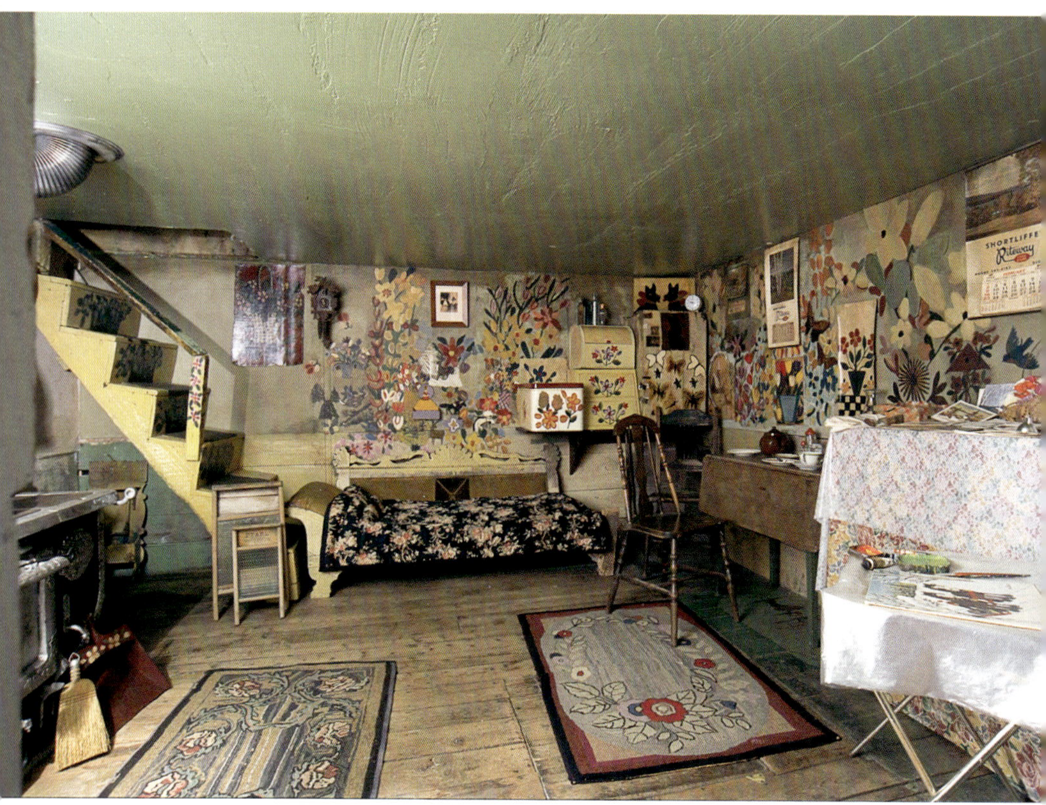

Wide angle view of the interior after restoration. (Gary Castle)

a "limited" life. Her temperament — creative, persevering, fun-oving, life-loving — is a gift to us through her home and work. I am very appreciative to all those who created a stream of efforts to conserve her tiny house that I was blessed enough to see/feel on my overnight stay in Halifax. Lovely, tender, humorous, human.

—Visitor, Philadelphia, Pennsylvania

Utterly charming and inspiring — what an example of a free, beautiful spirit in the confines of a limited body, a tiny house, and a simple, local life. Thank you so much for conserving this national treasure.

—Visitor, Toronto, Ontario

Thank you for bringing Maud Lewis's house here for all to see! We really enjoyed it! Your house is beautiful.

—Visitor, aged 9, Yarmouth, Nova Scotia

We used to live in Yarmouth in the 1960s and often drove by Maud's house (at its original site). We are very happy to see it here, safe and sound. Our children, now living in Ontario and Alberta, love "the little old house by the road."

—Visitor, Woodstock, Ontario

Glossary of Terms

Alkyd A synthetic resin derived from glycerol and phthalic anhydride and used in paints.

Aqueous Water-based.

Anneal Subject to heat and slow cooling so as to toughen and reduce brittleness.

BEVA 371 A reversible thermoplastic adhesive.

Chelating agent Any of several compounds capable of binding heavy metal ions, thereby preventing interaction between the bound ions and the rest of the medium.

Consolidation Treatment using an adhesive to re-attach localized areas of ground or paint.

Coroplast A corrugated polypropylene/polyethylene copolymer.

Craquelure A fine network of cracks in a painting.

Cross-section A minute sample taken perpendicular to the surface through multiple layers of a painting.

Fascia A flat, horizontal member between architectural mouldings.

Fills Additions of putty or gesso to even out a surface where loss has occurred.

Gusset A triangular insert of wood for strengthening.

Impasto The application of thick layers of pigment to a canvas or other surface in painting.

Inpainting The filling in of missing paint strictly within the borders of the loss.

Key A wedge-like device to lock together structural parts, as in securing plaster to wooden lath.

Lascaux 360 A reversible contact adhesive emulsion, a water dispersion of butyl methacrulate copolymer thickened with butyl polyacrylate.

Lath A narrow, thin strip of wood used in making a supporting structure for plaster.

Loss An area of missing paint revealing the ground or support beneath.

Microballoons Hollow phenolic spheres used as bulking material.

Patinate In this context, to apply a toned layer to simulate an aged look.

Photomicroscopy Taking of photographs through a microscope.

Polymerize Make two or more monomers unite to form a polymer.

Poultice A moist, soft mass of an adhesive substance.

Retouching Similar to inpainting; filling in of areas of paint loss with pigment and medium to match the surrounding original paint.

Ridge cap Horizontal board covering the join at the peak of a roof.

Scarf A joint formed by strapping two notched timbers together to make a continuous piece.

Scumble An overlay of opaque paint which has been thinned to a semi-transparent state.

Sheathing A layer of material applied to the outer frame of a building to strengthen the structure and serve as a base for an exterior weatherproof cladding.

Soffit The underside of a structural component.

Strainer A frame with fixed corners on which a canvas is stretched

Stud An upright post in the framework of a wall for supporting sheets of lath or wallboard.

Substrate Any layer of material carrying one or more layers of paint.

Surfactant A substance which reduces the surface tension of a liquid.

Thermosetting Permanently hardening or solidifying by heating.

Wainscotting Panelling, usually wood, applied to the lower part of the interior walls of a room.

Selected Bibliography

Arnold, Robert. "CCI Report on the Maud Lewis Painted House, Preliminary Condition Report." 25 April 1979.

Arnold, Robert. "CCI Report on an Examination of the Maud Lewis Painted House." 31 March 1981.

Baker, Victoria. *The Croscups' Painted Room*. Ottawa: National Gallery of Canada, 1990.

Barnard, Elissa. "Book Earnings to Aid Repair of Lewis Home." *Chronicle Herald*, 26 July 1996.

Barnard, Murray. "The Little Old Lady Who Paints Pretty Pictures." *Star Weekly*, 10 July 1965, pp. 12-15.

Courtney, Lisa. "Maude [sic] Lewis House becomes Cultural Artifact." *The Picaro*, 1 November 1984.

Cowan, Janet. "Dry Methods for Surface Cleaning of Paper." *CCI Technical Bulletin* No. 11, 1986.

Cropas, Nyna. "By the Window Painting." *Visual Arts News* 5:2 (Summer 1981), pp. 12-15.

Gaudet, J. Alan. "Report on the Maude [sic] Lewis Painted House Prepared for the Maude [sic] Lewis Painted House Society." February 1980.

Greenaway, Cora. "Maud's Folk Fantasies." *Century Home*, April 1988.

Hodkinson, Ian. "Conservation and Transfer of an Early 19th Century Painted Room." *Association for Preservation Technology Bulletin* 14:1 (1982), pp. 17-35.

Hume, Christopher. "Simple Power of Lewis." *Toronto Star*, 25 January 1998.

McElroy, Gil. "Sundays in the Gallery with Maud." *ArtsAtlantic* 58 (Summer 1997), pp. 30-32.

Pearse, Harold. "The Serial Imagery of Maud Lewis." *ArtsAtlantic* 58 (Summer 1997), pp. 26-29.

Pearse, Harold. "Folk Art: Classic, Neo, and Post." *Art Gallery of Nova Scotia Journal* 9 (September 1992 - February 1993), pp. 7-9.

Pinsent, Claudia. "The Joyful Gifts of Maud Lewis." *Atlantic Books Today* (Winter 1996/7).

Schlichting, Carl. "Working with Polyethylene Foam and Fluted Plastic Sheet." *CCI Technical Bulletin* No. 14, 1994.

Smulders, Marilyn. "Pretty Pictures." *Daily News*, 3 August 1995.

Telescope. "The Once-Upon-a-Time World of Maud Lewis." Canadian Broadcasting Corporation, 1965.

Wetmore, Bert. "Works on Doors, Walls, Windows, Even Kitchenware." *Halifax Herald*, 23 November 1950.

Woolaver, Lance. *The Illuminated Life of Maud Lewis*. Halifax: Nimbus and Art Gallery of Nova Scotia, 1997.

Contributors

Laurie Hamilton has been Fine Art Conservator at the Art Gallery of Nova Scotia for more than twenty years. A graduate of Queen's University with a Master of Art Conservation degree, she is responsible for the physical well being of the fine art objects in the collection of the Art Gallery of Nova Scotia. She supervised the overall restoration of the Maud Lewis House and its eventual installation in the Scotiabank Maud Lewis Gallery. As well as telling the story of this project, *The Painted House of Maud Lewis: Conserving a Folk Art Treasure* is illustrated in part by Hamilton's photographic documentation.

Jennifer McLaughlin is a Fine Art Conservator who teaches conservation and restoration at the London Guildhall University, London, England. She also maintains a private practice, Jennifer McLaughlin Fine Art Conservation, in Halifax, Nova Scotia. McLaughlin has a Master of Art Conservation degree from Queen's University and was primarily responsible for the treatment of the many painted artifacts related to the Maud Lewis Painted House restoration.

Craig Dix is an Artifact Conservator working in private practice. His business, Atlantic Heritage Preservation, is in Halifax, Nova Scotia. Trained at Algonquin College, Dix has worked for the Manitoba Museum of Man and Nature, the Nova Scotia Museum and Parks Canada. Specializing in the treatment of furniture and wooden objects, Dix and his team tackled the structural aspects of the Painted House restoration.

Index

Page references to illustrations appear in italics.

This book was designed and typeset by Neil Meister,
Semaphor Design Company Inc., with art direction
by Julie Scriver, Goose Lane Editions.

Text is typeset in Adobe Bembo® 12pt.
Display type is typeset in Adobe Berthold Bodoni® Antiqua.
The paper is Luna Matte 200M.
Colour separations by Maritime Digital Colour Inc.
Printed and bound in Canada by Friesens.